Frazzled *Hurried* Woman!

Frazzled
Hurried
Woman!

· ·

Your Stress Relief Guide to Thriving...
Not Merely Surviving

ROSALIE MOSCOE

Health in Harmony
Toronto, ON, Canada

Illustration concepts by Rosalie Moscoe
Illustrations by Bojan Redzic

Library and Archives Canada Cataloguing in Publication

Moscoe, Rosalie
Frazzled, hurried woman! : your stress relief guide
to thriving-- not merely surviving / Rosalie Moscoe.

Includes bibliographical references.
Issued also in electronic formats.
ISBN 978-0-9880138-0-3

1. Stress management for women. I. Title.

RA785.M675 2012   155.9'042082   C2012-902106-7

ISBN: 978-0-9880138-0-3

Health In Harmony
842 Eglinton Avenue West, Unit No. 85557
Toronto, Ontario, M5N 0A2
Canada
Rosalie@healthinharmony.com
www.healthinharmony.com

Printed in Canada

I dedicate this book to my daughter Rhonda, a thriving, successful yet sensitive and loving woman.

Rhonda, you have always brought me joy. Throughout your life, I hope you continue to keep that delicate balance of satisfying your personal potential, yet still being available when you can for others. Hopefully your next generation of women (my precious granddaughter Aliyah included) will avoid the pitfalls of The Frazzled Hurried Woman.

Love always,
Mum

What People are Saying about Frazzled Hurried Woman!

Frazzled Hurried Woman! is a comprehensive wellness book that goes far beyond just stress management. Both accessible and highly informative, it is an excellent guide for the general public, students and professionals.

As a valuable on-going resource, it would make an excellent addition to the recommended reading list for anyone studying stress management and personal well-being in post-secondary educational institutions.

Rosalie combines the power of storytelling with sound research and practical applications to help readers find their way in their quest for balance, despite often hectic, challenging and overwhelming periods in their lives.

This is a thoughtful, practical, engaging and entertaining book that helps readers change their behaviors and perceptions in order to enhance their life journeys.

Coreen Flemming, Professor and Coordinator,
Workplace Wellness and Health Promotion at Centennial College, '88-'08
2008 Health, Work and Wellness Pioneer Award recipient.

Rosalie does it again!

This book is wonderful. Every chapter is packed with practical, easy to follow advice for the (overworked) modern woman. Changing your life is hard. Rosalie almost makes it easy, by explaining why change is necessary, and providing numerous simple examples for places to start, and offering sound medical explanations. Rosalie pulls no punches. The stories she tells from her private life are courageous and inspiring. I'd love to send this book to all my patients.

Dr. M. Zitney, MD, DAAPM

Chronic Pain Specialist

Headache & Pain Relief Centre, Toronto, Canada

www.headachepainreliefcentre.ca

Rosalie Moscoe is my kind of author. She is upbeat, accurate and orthomolecular. I recommend her new book, **Frazzled Hurried Woman!** (unless, somehow, you'd prefer to be frazzled and hurried). If you think you are too busy to read it, that's why you need it.

Andrew W. Saul, PhD

Assistant Editor, Journal of Orthomolecular Medicine; Author of *Doctor Yourself* and *Orthomolecular Medicine for Everyone*; Editor of Orthomolecular Medicine News Service.

www.DoctorYourself.com

Stop right here. Ladies, it's time to attend to your well-being. Rest your tired back on a comfy cushion and enjoy **Frazzled Hurried Woman!** It was written for overworked women just like you because Rosalie knows that your lives are plagued with demands.

Every chapter offers comforting advice for managing busy days. In charming style, this resourceful author consistently weaves academic research with common sense and real experience to help you renew your sense of self.

As a high energy, empathetic and intelligent individual, an entertainer, a volunteer, fundraiser and professional speaker who lives in a modern, fast-paced city, Rosalie understands well the daily frustrations invoked by fatigue. She's a mom, a wife,

a youthful grandmother and every woman's mentor for good health. Love this book. Take it to heart. It's a clear wake-up call.
C.K. Clarke, BA BEd, writing consultant ccink@sympatico.ca

Frazzled Hurried Woman! was written with a compassionate, playful, and loving spirit; its vivid illustrations communicate powerfully. Rosalie's advice is balanced and psychologically sound. You will quickly discover yourself in the pages of her book especially through her poetry and quotes. I encourage you to read *The Modern Day Woman's Lament*, on page 34: 'I straddle the precipice between work and home.'

A comprehensive and substantive coverage of 11 key areas of daily living with clear and concrete practical tips each step along the way, written in a down-to-earth and action-oriented approach, **Frazzled Hurried Woman!** is easy to read, understand and put into action. I particularly enjoyed the practical information Rosalie researched about healthy food, nutrition and eating. So wonderful, having Rosalie's key ideas and work concisely pulled together in one place.

I have been inspired by Rosalie's work for over 10 years. She is a sincere, authentic, warm and inviting woman, rich in life experience, with many and varied talents and gifts. Rosalie is a remarkable person, woman, mother, wife and human being as well as an engaging, sensitive, enthusiastic, powerful, creative and passionate professional.

I can't wait for the CD version of the book to play in my car with Rosalie's music and singing. Rosalie's **Frazzled Hurried Woman!** speaks powerfully to me in the important areas of my life.
Dr. Jim Leonidas PhD, C. Psych. Registered Psychologist
Email: jimleonidas@mac.com.
Toronto, Ontario, Canada

Rosalie Moscoe's **Frazzled Hurried Woman!** is a must-read for anyone feeling overcommitted, overextended and overwhelmed and for the people who love them. This wise, delightful and sensitive book clearly defines the problems and provides creative solutions and great tips: fear and anger exercises, breathing techniques, ways to self-soothe, identifying personal needs and wants, how we can choose to use our energy. Rosalie's warm and charming writing style are so very enjoyable as are the wonderful illustrations. Best of all, this book offers CHOICES. What a gift that is when it feels like there's no way out.

Elayne Savage, PhD, speaker, Psychotherapist,
coach and author of, *Don't Take it Personally! The Art of Dealing with Rejection; Breathing Room – Creating Space to Be a Couple*
www.QueenofRejection.com
Email: elayne@QueenofRejection.com, Ph: 510-540-6258

Just What the Doctor Ordered!

Rosalie Moscoe's e-book, **Frazzled Hurried Woman!** is a prescription for serenity. So many women today are at their wit's end juggling multiple accountabilities. They do their best to satisfy the overflowing needs of spouse, partners, children, career, friends and associates. Rosalie, a long-time speaker, health expert, and entertainer, cracks the code. She shares simple, down-to-earth strategies for reclaiming sanity and balance, all while serving the interests of those in her world . . . starting with herself. 5 Stars!

Burt Dubin, president, Personal Achievement Institute,
www.SpeakingSuccess.com
Email: burt@burtdubin.com Ph: 928-753-5315

ACKNOWLEDGEMENTS

Writing this book has been an inspiring process for me personally.

To **Ray Moscoe**, my dear husband, long-time partner in life. You have always been there for me, supporting my career choices. You never seemed to mind the long nights I spent at the computer writing this book, and your loving reminders to listen to my own advice always brought me back to center. Thanks for your opinions about subjects in this book that always made a difference and only added to the end product. I also wish to thank my daughter **Rhonda Moscoe**, my son-in-law **Michael Meade**, and my son **Darren Moscoe** for their support, love and excitement for all my work. Along with my granddaughter **Aliyah** and husband Ray, all of you have provided me with insight into love and life; you have allowed me an awareness and profound richness of life that would never have been there without all of you.

I wish to give thanks to people who have helped me along the way. **Judy Cullins**, www.bookcoaching.com, gave me some great strategies regarding format, style and organization of a book and e-book. Thanks Judy for your spirited and expert coaching about all aspects of writing, marketing and chapter formatting. Thanks to **Tsufit**, business coach and author of *Step into the Spotlight*, who also gave me great ideas for this second edition to enhance the product.

Also crucial to this book project was **Carol Clarke**, my dedicated writing consultant. Thanks Carol for your expertise, caring and keen use of the English language. Your valuable suggestions helped me to polish my work chapter by chapter. Many thanks to **Pat Startek**, expert proofreader, and to **Raj Sanduja**, my key communications and project assistant.

The fun, brilliant illustrations that enliven my copy I owe to **Bojan Redzic**, sbredzic@sympatico.ca, illustrator extraordinaire! Thanks Bojan for capturing my ideas in writing and crafting them into colorful, lively, expert cartoon illustrations. Truly, a picture is worth a thousand words!

To **Tania Craan**, typesetting and book cover designer, whose presentation so beautifully showcases my work. Thanks for your great style and ideas.

To **Burt Dubin**, burtdubin.com, my long-time speaking coach, thank you Burt for your help and ideas for marketing this product. But more than that, you first made me think about "the spirit and passion of the speaker." You led me to the questioning of what it is I'm trying to say through my speaking and my writing. Those exercises led me to deepen my introspection of what I want to leave as my legacy. Your ability to stir my thinking was instrumental in the creation of this work.

To my **dear friends** and other **supportive family members**, thanks for all your enthusiasm, support, lessons on life and for your love. You have encouraged me towards self growth and prompted me to assist others to find fulfillment from within. I am truly blessed.

FOREWORD by Dr. Abram Hoffer, MD, PhD

There are few books that cover the whole field of what we have to do and how to live in order to deal with stress and with the vicissitudes of normal life. The only way to live productive interesting lives is to remain well. This book, in amazing detail, tells us how. It will not be on the best sellers' list of Big Pharma whose greatest fear is a population of well people who seldom have to take any drugs. Is this possible? Yes, Mrs. Moscoe thinks it is and I agree with her. This conclusion is based upon my own experience of being a psychiatrist for nearly 58 years and still being able to practice as a consultant in nutrition at age 90, as well as having had to deal with the tragedies and losses of family and friends.

Based upon thousands of patients and, more recently, clients I have seen over the years, there is no doubt that what Rosalie Moscoe wrote is excellent advice. The body is so amazing: given the right tools (food and supplements) it can restore itself even from the most miserable of conditions to good health and activity. Having seen chronic schizophrenic patients after decades of illness become well, having seen patients with severe depression recover without drugs which had not helped them, having seen thousands of children lose their hyperactivity, lose their irritability, lose their learning disorders and become normal, happy and active without Ritalin, I can assure you that the information in this book is right on. Had I known as much in 1955 as I know now and what Moscoe describes so thoroughly and well, my results would have been even better and achieved more quickly and I would have prescribed drugs even less frequently.

The basic elements of normal life, which nature has taken billions of years to establish, are having the nutritional tools with which to heal oneself and having enough energy to deal with stress and to live actively. We have been adapted for activity which has been life saving—as when we were being chased or we're chasing for our lives and food. We also can't live in isolation and need understanding, companionship and a feeling that we are needed and helpful to others. Our mission in life should be to remain well, and to work on behalf of humanity. This book, **Frazzled Hurried Woman!** will help us achieve that end. Men too become frazzled and hurried. I recommend they read this book as well.

Abram Hoffer, MD, PhD (1917 − 2009), psychiatrist, author of over 30 books and over 600 research papers, Past President Emeritus, The International Schizophrenia Foundation and Journal of Orthomolecular Medicine, www.orthomed.org. and 50 years of vitamin research, practice and publication.

TABLE OF CONTENTS

INTRODUCTION
Welcome to seekers of stress relief and well-being!

Today in North America, millions of women experience "frazzled" symptoms due to trying to juggle many roles within family, work and community. For the most part the Frazzled Woman is excited by her life, yet there never seems to be enough time to do everything. She is always in a hurry! Does this sound like you? You are capable and involved, but often rushed off your feet to the point of exhaustion. Your moods fluctuate and you agonize over your lack of physical (and emotional) fitness. Every morning, you want to pull the covers over your head and go back to sleep.

If you are rushed, frazzled and live as though you are careening through your days on a high-speed, runaway roller coaster, I'm glad you found your way to this book. Within these pages, you are offered hope, help and ways to access natural healing.

**Frazzled Hurried Woman! Your Stress Relief Guide to Striving....
Not Merely Surviving** gives you comforting, easy solutions to
quiet the turmoil and find calm. You'll identify your stressors,
learn how to set boundaries and recover your sleep patterns.
The circles under your eyes will subside along with the nagging feeling in the pit of your stomach that "something isn't
right." People might even ask you if you've had a face lift!

Yes, Frazzled Woman, for me "something wasn't right"! I
spent years with throat infections, back problems and other
ailments. I was on puffers, antibiotics, and in back therapy.
Nothing seemed to help. I finally decided to take charge of
my life. I'm glad I did. I learned ways to relax, to improve my
diet, my lifestyle and most importantly, to alter my attitudes.
In doing so, I boosted my health and well-being. I feel better
today than I did 25 years ago and I am sharing all my best
recovery knowledge with you.

So here we are together. We will review the dilemmas that
Frazzled Women face, and I'll show you how to manage them
and win! You can read the chapters in the order they are presented or choose to read what suits you at the moment. It's
time to put on the brakes and step safely off that roller coaster!

Rosalie Moscoe, RHN, RNCP
Toronto, Ontario, Canada

CHAPTER ONE

Overcommitment and Stress

Frazzled Woman in a hurry, I know you well!

I too was once a walking zombie, burdened by too many responsibilities. I felt guilty, depressed, alone and trapped. My energy sapped, I had to push myself into every task.

Stress was my idea of fun; I loved it, or thought I did because I was under the illusion that I was being productive by being busy—always. Can you relate?

That attitude goes back a long way. In my case, I can recall my grade five teacher threatening our class of 9 and 10 year old children every morning, her face stern and one long finger pointed at us. "Keep yourselves busy," she'd warn. It was a crime to be idle, to daydream, to (heaven forbid) look out the window. That was an early glimpse into our work-oriented society, since being busy has long been equated with achievement. There is no respect for the unsuccessful life. And so we race ourselves into fatigue.

Being worn out and rushed isn't living; it's merely surviving.

According to the American Psychological Association's 2007 *Stress in America Survey*, mothers in the 'sandwich generation,' ages 35-54, feel more stress than any other age group as they balance the demanding delicate acts of caring for growing children and their aging parents.

Stress is the main underlying culprit for symptoms of the Frazzled Woman. The root causes are found in juggling family and work responsibilities: concern for your children's futures, for financial stability—the latter always fixed to your career and its demands. Not to be ignored is your need for acceptance and recognition at home, on the job and in the community. We are always striving to keep up with our own agendas.

Many women are frustrated with the situation, but don't know what to do about it. They simply keep forcing one weary step after another, from right after the alarm clock blares in the morning, often until everyone else is bedded down for the night. And all the time, they wear brave, capable faces. Sound familiar? You wouldn't be reading this book if you weren't in their ranks. You expect a lot of yourself on a daily basis, don't you?

Stress and Overstress

A normal level of stress heightens your senses and stimulates your energy. It keeps you challenged and on your toes. If you have an important project, you're challenged; your brain is actually growing more connections.

When a cat faces a threat, its claws emerge, its fur stands on end and its pupils dilate. So too, when we are threatened, our hearts beat faster, our metabolisms surge. The hypothalamus, a tiny pea-shaped gland in our brains, sends signals to the endocrine and nervous systems to speed up. Senses heightened, we're ready for a fight or flight. That stress reaction is normal, and meant to be short-lived. After the crisis, the body needs time to rest and recuperate in order to return to homeostasis, its natural state.

The 'father' of stress research, Hans Selye, M.D, famous research scientist, first introduced the concept of 'stress' as an explanation for the body's reaction to extraordinary circumstances. According to Selye, stress is "the non-specific response of the body to any demand placed upon it." It is an orchestrated set of bodily defenses known as The General Adaptation Syndrome, as follows:

1. an alarm reaction (biological changes in the body), followed by . . .
2. a stage of resistance. The body tries to cope with the stressor. If the stress continues, it is followed by . . .
3. a stage of exhaustion.

Overstress appears as exhaustion, an inability to cope. You cannot accept any more stimulation. Even going out with friends can seem like a chore. Repetitive stress taxes mind and body, as the 'switch' that turns the stress response on and off starts to malfunction. In a 'frazzled' state due to repetitive stressors—worry, traffic jams, too many responsibilities, kids, work, poor diet, and lack of other healthy lifestyle choices—the stress response turns on way too often. It hasn't been given the chance to shut down for a rest as nature intended.

Eventually, the endocrine and sympathetic nervous systems that prepare for the stress response wear down as they become **overtaxed** from **overstress.**

The Frazzled Woman, the one who copes with repetitive stress, looks tense and tired. Her eyes are puffy and circled. She can't focus too long on any one conversation, often thinking other thoughts while you talk to her. She gets into accidents. She loses things: files, keys, perhaps her wallet. Sooner or later she may lose her sense of self.

Constant rushing and living the harried life may also lead to physical disorders such as backache, stomach problems, or IBS (irritable bowel syndrome). IBS, PMS, and you're a mess! Your immune system starts to suffer. You come down with one cold or virus after another. But there's more!

Overstress causes high blood pressure, cardiovascular disease, headaches, irritability and insomnia. This leads to overeating especially of high fat or foods loaded with carbohydrates: chocolate, bread, potatoes—comfort foods. When women are stressed, fat accumulates on the abdomen (This layer of fat is supposed to be ready fuel for the liver in times of stress for the 'fight or flight' response. We are excessively prepared!).

Want to Make a Change?

Know that humans have a body-mind connection. Scientists tell us that our thoughts affect our mental or physical health. In addition, your perception of what is stressful is purely personal. Someone else may not even give your idea of a stressful event a second thought. Many of our stressors today are psychological and based on what we fret about. Yet stress chemicals still prepare us to meet the enemy, and when they're released too often, cause collective damage. Consider your tense shoulders, neck pain and knotted stomach. You really don't have to endure them. Much of your day is no doubt physically demanding. It's that double whammy, the exhausted mind and body, that's sinking you.

Let's start with a quick, honest self-assessment:
a) Are you tired and unfocused?
b) Do you have trouble losing (or gaining) weight?
c) Are you often moody and 'down' a lot?
d) Are your relationships stormy?
e) Are you having many negative thoughts and feelings?
f) Is your sex drive stalling?
g) Have your physical problems and illnesses increased?
h) Do you notice an increase in bad habits?

You can stop nodding your head now. You know where you are, so visualize **where you want to be**. Close your eyes and imagine yourself as calm and happy, with a life that's in harmony. Notice how you look with that new contented expression on your face. Use the ideas in this chapter to help you get there.

Starting to Take Control of Your Runaway Life

Keep a journal. You can either consider it your secret diary and stash it in a drawer or keep the details in your mind (if there's room left!). This should not be a burdensome task.

Either jot down a heading called **Present Commitments** and list them (or think about them. Count them on your fingers if need be!).

Don't forget duties beyond work and home. Are you also committed to volunteer work?

What about commitment to yourself? **Are you ready to add your name to the list?**

When you review your list, do you feel accomplished, energized and challenged? Or do you feel overwhelmed, tired, and wonder how you manage to do it all? You may ask yourself questions such as: "Why didn't I ask for a half-time teaching load after two years of feeling exhausted?"

You may not feel you can do everything you've listed, yet you can and you do—although how well do you **cope**?

Decide which commitments you can drop. We've become highly task-oriented and pack our calendars by the hour and minute. It's as though we won't make it to the next day if we don't complete everything NOW! Ask yourself, is this true? Do you think you're **supposed** to do all these things?

Who said so?

This is not about abandoning your responsibilities, but remembering your responsibility to your own needs. It's recognizing and honoring your limits so you can be the best you can be to your family, your work, your community and to yourself.

The 'Must Do It All' Generation

In the 1980's we were told we could have it all. That led to our **doing it all**. While many would say we're a 'must have it all' generation, I believe we're 'must do it all' junkies. Because of that attitude, we are **overcommitted**. Most of our ancestors worked many years to achieve what today's generation wants **immediately**.

Can we learn delayed gratification, that is, to wait another week or two, or even another year, before we have everything? Can we be content to enjoy what we can manage in the moment? Notice whether your habit of overcommitment follows a set pattern from the last generation. Ingrained habits die hard.

Six Steps to Combat Overcommitment:
1. Outline your priorities.

You'll want to keep most of your commitments, but even those you consider high priority can be pared down or some parts delegated. From the remaining items in your list of Present Commitments, pick one obligation you can you drop right away, or soon. For example, you may be a volunteer as minute taker for a social club. Ask yourself—can I let go of this?

If it's not that important to your life or at the bottom of the list, consider letting it go.

Are you a perfectionist? If so, you want the job done right and you have to do it **yourself. You want things done a certain way.** Perfectionists often try to micro-manage the small things. Perfectionism looms high in people who are over-committed. Resolve to loosen your perfectionist habits.

Make this statement your new mantra: **I will do one thing imperfectly every day.**

2. Ask for help!

For which tasks can you delegate all or part of the job? Consider the following: get someone to pick up the kids instead of your always doing it or get the family to help with cleaning up at home. Or, if you can, hire a cleaning lady. The money you spend will be worth your time and energy. Prefer to do **all** your own cleaning? Get over it. Assign logical chores to family members. Children will take to cleaning if they know how it's done: 'stuff' either gets tossed, put somewhere else or neatly returned to its current location. Kids can fold towels, dust tables or walk the dog, depending on their age and abilities. Start them young. Sloppy teenage habits are hard to reverse.

Likely you will find it difficult to give up or delegate anything. You feel you should be able to do everything and still cope. You think the more you do the happier you will be, yet the more you do, the more overwhelmed you feel. Happiness is nowhere in sight. You tell yourself, "I'll take a break later, when I'm finished all my chores," but you're never finished.

Take a break. Be kind to yourself. There will always be something to finish—that's life. It's time to face your Frazzled Woman symptoms and feel human again.

3. Dissect one of your most stressful commitments.

Your stress may come from a combination of all of your commitments. For now, just choose one that stands out in your mind. To tackle them all at once may cause further feelings of being overwhelmed.

Your own thoughts and feelings about what is expected of you for each of your responsibilities will determine how much stress you will feel. Expectations of others factor into demands for your time.

a) Eldercare: There is a certain emotional drive to care for aging parents that can tax us like no other output of energy.

Speaking from personal experience, there comes a point in every caregiver's life when enough is enough. The condition is well known as 'burnout.' Caregivers often become overwhelmed; they experience anxiety, depression and exhaustion. Extreme stress, the culprit that undermines the immune system, makes our bodies more susceptible to illness. In his published book, *Handbook of Human Stress and Immunity*, Robert

Bonneau, assistant professor of microbiology and immunology at Penn State's Hershey Medical Center, emphasizes that stress does affect overall health. He notes that "the brain, the immune system and the endocrine system, which secretes hormones, all talk to one another." His study includes lymphocytes, the infection-fighting white blood cells produced by the immune system in response to stress.

Have you ever come down with a cold or flu after a significant stressful event? A cousin of mine became very tired and run down while caring for his dear wife, a multiple sclerosis patient. His immune system, under siege, had a difficult time fighting off invading viruses and bacteria. During this emotionally draining period in his life, he contracted Hepatitis C. Both partners had to be hospitalized.

Caring for others is tricky business and requires careful balance. If you're not caring for yourself, you may be compromising your ability to care for anyone else. I've seen daughters frantic enough to yell at an ailing parent. Facing unrelenting stress, they became too distraught to realize that their own emotional or physical health was suffering.

A number of years ago, while I was still working, taking courses and caring for my family, I was chief caregiver for my father. My dad suffered from the complications of diabetes. Although he still lived at home with his wife, she was having trouble coping. Therefore, I was appointed 'Staff Sergeant.' For the most part, I was the one who took him to doctor and hospital appointments, picked up his prescriptions and kept watch on his diet.

Even after Dad lost a leg to diabetes and was living in a nursing home, I was still the one making the decisions about his care. I was the family member who shopped for his clothing and continued to accompany him to hospital appointments.

While I was doing all these things out of love and duty as a daughter, increasingly my multiple roles became a juggling act. I began to feel overwhelmed, wavering between resentment and guilt.

Finally, I was exhausted and admitted to myself that I needed help. Despite my desire to be in control, I was clearly off course in this particular situation. Fortunately, the workers at the social services agency for seniors were able to steer me in a positive direction. They understood my dilemma and had the resources to help.

According to the American Psychiatric Association, if you are a caregiver, it's essential to monitor yourself so that you eat properly, get adequate sleep, continue to socialize and do something you enjoy. Normal life events are a necessary break from the rigors of caring for someone with an illness or disability. You'll be better able to face your responsibility with a sense of calmness. With a better frame of mind your energy and hope will return.

Some of your strategies might include:
- recruiting family members to help with chores
- calling agencies that can give care
- arranging a 'Meals on Wheels' program
- considering a short or long term care facility for your loved one

If you are in a helping profession and also care for a sick relative, you're in double jeopardy. I urge you to recognize your limits. Have the same compassion for yourself as you have for those you may counsel. Talk to your colleagues and receive support from one another. It's likely that you are aware of these strategies, but when people are suffering undue stress, they often forget to do what they already know. Furthermore, some people may feel guilty if they have fun or enjoy themselves when those they love are suffering.

I urge you to do something to ease the stress of being a caregiver. The health of both you and your family members depend on it. Don't wait until you're at your wit's end!

b) Volunteer/Employee: Volunteering whether with a local charity or teaching Sunday school can be a joy, a passion, yet another commitment. Have you offered too much of yourself?

If your most stressful commitment happens to be (paid) work, do you feel you're getting fairly compensated? Do you feel your job is meaningful in some way, perhaps by helping others? Is the issue your relationship with your supervisor or boss? Can you think of ways to improve your situation if you're feeling overworked, underpaid or undervalued? Perhaps you need to take upgrading courses or ask for a raise.

Maybe you need to speak to your boss or supervisor about something that concerns your control with your duties. According to the Addiction and Research Foundation, feeling a lack of power over your work is a major reason for work-related stress and depression.

Your Frazzled Woman's Rescue Mentor says: We really need to love our work—or at least something about it!

Identify some strategies you can take to improve your work situation (example: talk to your supervisor about more leeway for deadlines). **Very often, deadlines are not really final.** For instance, that report that you may have worked on well into several nights so that it's ready on deadline may actually sit on someone's desk for a week after you hand it in.

c) Children: Parenting, without a doubt, is very demanding especially if you have a child with learning difficulties, illness or behavior problems. While you can't let go of your responsibilities, what you can do is analyze how to start controlling your stress levels about them. Professional advice can be liberating. A visit with the teacher, the family doctor or the counseling office at school can be revealing. When you ask, you may find surprising help available.

Working full-time and parenting is a major source of discussion among young mothers today. Given the large number of women in the workforce, obviously women want or need to work for mental stimulation, career and personal development, and/or financial gain. However with pressing demands of home life (especially if a women has three or more children), it isn't easy to harmonize work and children. Women are increasingly asking employers for flexible hours, deciding to work part-time instead of full-time, or delaying re-entering the workforce until children are older. Each woman needs to examine what is best for herself and her family.

4. Turn your overnurturer button to 'off' mode.

Do friends ask you to take them to the airport? Think of the time it takes, the hassle of heavy traffic, especially if it's in rush hour.

'ON' is our modern disease. Ask yourself if you really want to do the task requested of you. Often the same people will keep asking you to do things for them. They will stop asking if you say NO often enough. Don't worry, they'll find someone else to do it.

If it's your adult children or parents who are asking for the ride, you can reconsider and do it. Or you can tell them the truth—that you're overburdened. If you still want to help and if you can really afford it, you can always offer to pay for a taxi cab or an airport limo.

Overnurturers take on too much without giving it much

thought. I implore you to stop and think about why you take on so much. Likely, the reasons are multiple.

Check which overnurturer traits apply to you:

✓ You try to be "Everything to Everybody."[1] You're likely an overachiever as well. Once you've taken on a responsibility, you can't let people down by backing out.

✓ You have a superman/woman mentality and haven't learned how to set limits.

✓ Pleasing others is a chance to prove yourself. It's a bit of a high.

✓ Your self-esteem is at stake. You feel you should be able to accomplish more in a day. If you can't, you push even harder to prove to yourself that you can do it.

Did you check off most of the above? The problem is that the harder you push to accomplish, the more stressed, depressed, tired and depleted you become. You may try to excel in multiple roles and are the victim of your own success. But therein lies the trap: the more a woman shows she can do, the more others demand of her. The cost to your physical and mental health? Enormous!

You cannot be everything to everyone. Primary relationships often suffer when fatigue creates bad moods; workaholism is a major reason for marital break up. Enjoyment of life becomes a wash out. Are we having fun yet? Don't give up the ship. It is possible to harmonize your life and feel human again.

5. Practice saying NO.

This next week, practice saying NO to any new commitments. This may **not** work if the request is work-related. "Sorry boss,

---

1. H. B. Braiker, Ph.D. *The Type E* Woman*, Dodd, Mead & Company, 1989, p. 5.

I can't take on the job; I'm in a stress program and I'm practicing saying NO." Not sure if that would go over so well.

But there are things you can say to a supervisor or boss if you're already overwhelmed at work. Example: "If I take on this new project now, I may have put aside projects # 1, 2, and 3. Which one has priority? What dates do you need all of them by?" As I mentioned, very often deadlines are not absolute.

Start to notice if your switch is always turned ON. You're just raring to do something for somebody. That state of 'other-person-readiness' distracts from what you have to do for yourself.

Don't overcommit. Do you feel guilty saying NO? Feeling guilty (or remorseful) is appropriate in situations when we may have behaved badly, so we can know when to amend mistakes. However, feeling guilty especially in situations when we're overwhelmed due to overcommitment can cripple us and run or ruin our lives. If you routinely take on others' problems and responsibilities, learn to disengage gracefully. If you don't, you're making their issues more important than your own.

"If you must love your neighbor as yourself, it makes just as good sense to love yourself as your neighbor."
— *Nicholas de Chamfort, 18th Century French writer*

6. Practice saying YES to your own needs. Do something for yourself this next week, something you enjoy. Set aside at least 15 minutes a day to relax. Start treating yourself as well as you would treat others. Walk more slowly.

Schedule a physical check-up. Your feelings of being tired, exhausted or depressed may have physical origins. Make sure you have blood pressure and blood lipid (cholesterol and other fats in the blood) and iron levels taken. Ask for a urinalysis to rule out blood sugar problems. Have your hormone levels evaluated. Stress can often play havoc with female hormone levels. Your estrogen, progesterone, testosterone and/or DHEA levels may need balancing. Find a doctor who knows about bio-identical hormones to discuss hormone balance for symptom relief. See **Chapter 11, Menopause! A Change Like No Other** for more information on this subject.

You don't have to fix everything on your commitment list. Choose one or two items on the list you feel you can work on and develop an action plan for them. Resolve this week to make at least one change. Know that you deserve to be rid of symptoms of the Frazzled Woman. If you feel that some people are taking advantage of you, either reduce the number of commitments (by one) or the time you spend on them.

Take-Away Gems

1. Make a list of all your commitments. Drop something if you can, or ask for help. It really is okay.
2. Practice one or more of the 6 steps to combat overcommitment. Notice if your switch is always ON, that is, set to overnurturing. Carve out some time for yourself this week—even 15 minutes a day. Relax or indulge in some activity that you enjoy, perhaps going for a walk.
3. Notice when you are rushing. Make an effort to slow your pace.
4. Schedule a physical check-up.

You're On Your Way!

Bravo! You've reviewed your stressors and decided to tend to your physical health. Know that you have made the first important steps to transform your life from frazzled to fantastic!

The Modern Day Woman's Lament

I straddle the precipice between work and home.
The earth shifts beneath me and
Sometimes I think I'll split in two.
Loving my work, loving my family . . .
It shouldn't be a conflict, but often it is.
I want so much to be there for others,
For those I love, for myself
But my work draws me, taking on
A life of its own.

And like an addict I can't quit.
In denial, I take on more.
My back may hurt, my heart may pound
But still I surge forward,
Needing to accomplish, to succeed
With precision and excellence
To make a contribution
That I know a woman is capable of making.

There are days when all I want
Is to feel a cool breeze on my face
Sunlight on my shoulders
To hear children's laughter
To dance with abandon in the moonlight
Or listen to peaceful or enchanting music
Without guilt.

I accept the fact that a
Happy life is a balanced life.
Yet I still search and long

For that seemingly elusive balance
That can bring with it
A feeling of satisfaction and peace.

So today, I turn my face toward the sunlight
With hope and love for the day
And a sense of fun in my heart.
Like a circus juggler nimble and accurate,
When ultimately one of the balls is dropped…

I gather strength to accept the stark reality
Of that inevitable fumble.
With quiet acceptance and self compassion
I encounter the beauty of that moment
As perfection falls away and joyfulness enters.

by Rosalie Moscoe

CHAPTER TWO

Stress–It's All in Your Head

Are you too often negative?

Do you dislike the way you look?

Are you hard on yourself?

Do you feel jinxed, that bad things will happen to you?

You find yourself in a state of "Nothing good will happen to me," "Another day, another dollar," "I can't wait until the weekend" or "TGIF—Thank goodness it's Friday!" You wish your days away. You put a damper on your experiences and your very life.

In this chapter, you will discover that you can alter your perception of events.

We rush and remain harried to prevent ourselves the down-time to think, to review our pace and quality of life. We are afraid to hear our own thoughts because they are mostly negative.

It's natural to be joyful. When you were a child, do you remember how excited you felt on a rainy day? You pulled on your boots and gloriously splashed through puddles. It was the best fun. Today you look out of the window and see rain falling and think, "Stupid rain, it will ruin my new coat. I'll have to juggle my umbrella, my brief case, and my purse. What a drag!" You get to work and everyone grumbles about the crummy weather. You chime in.

What happened? Where did that little kid go with her sparkle and fun-loving nature? Beaten down by negativity, she lost her self-confidence and allowed people to criticize her. That's what happened to that little kid. She lost her joy.

Unless babies are hungry, wet or in pain, they are joyful human beings. By two months old, most are smiling and laughing. Young children laugh about 200 times a day. Adults are lucky to laugh 15 times a day. Are we too worried or stressed to laugh? Probably. Negative thoughts strangle passion and enthusiasm. Don't let that happen. Embrace your passion and enthusiastic responses! Keep them alive! They are the 'goodies' of life! Without them our days become mundane and lackluster. It is possible to find a smile for your face once again. Mood has a lot to do with our thoughts.

"There is nothing either good or bad,
but thinking makes it so."
— William Shakespeare

What is stressful for you may not make someone else blink an eye. It depends on you. First there must be an event or situation which is perceived by the mind as undesirable or threatening. Then the stress response with all its biological changes takes hold. The threat in your mind can be real or imagined. **Your body doesn't know the difference.**

Perception, Perception, Perception

Sara enters her workplace and walks down the hall not looking at or speaking to anyone. John, a co-worker, passes Sara and notices her blank, tense stare. He assumes she's preoccupied or upset about something and doesn't think about it again. Another co-worker, Judy, notices Sara's demeanor and immediately becomes offended and worried. Judy starts thinking, "What's the matter with her anyway? Is she angry with me? Did I say something yesterday to upset her?" She discusses the event with other co-workers and dwells on the incident the entire morning.

Judy worries that she has lost a friend. Her body feels a threat, causing her stress response to take hold. Her blood pressure begins to rise, her heart beats wildly and more cholesterol circulates in her system. Her palms feel sweaty. Her stomach does somersaults. This is the mind-body connection in full gear.

Judy gathers up the courage to confront Sara. It turns out Sara had a stomach ache that morning and was heading quickly for the ladies room. Moral of the story: Don't assume people are angry at you, ticked off or holding grudges. You can always ask, so to worry about it and raise your stress levels isn't worth it. As well as causing herself an unnecessary upset, Judy also wasted three hours of her employer's time!

Real or perceived, your stress response is the same. If you see a wind-up toy mouse dashing around the floor and you think it's real, your body will react correspondingly. Your heart will start to pound and your breathing will increase. You'll enter the fight/flight response to deal with the crisis. This is Nature's way to protect us, by giving us added strength when we need it. When more adrenaline and cortisol are produced, we can tackle the enemy or run faster. As the threat subsides, our bodies return to homeostasis, normal functioning. (Many people, especially those with road rage, live as though they constantly see mice dashing in their paths!)

Most women I know facing a mouse darting around on the floor, real or imagined, would run instead of fight. (I personally believe mice should only be seen in cartoon form on TV.) If you're the fighting type, you might grab something to strike it or think of a way to catch it live and remove it from the area. Either way, the stress response would still occur in your body. However, if you were raised on a farm and were used to seeing field mice, your perception of events would be different. You would likely be able to easily solve the problem. You would wonder what everyone was getting so upset about.

The Mind and Body Connection

Is the physical body all there is? No. There is more. Humans are equipped with a mind, body and spirit connection.

Do you blame your body for a neck ache? Maybe someone's a pain in the neck to you. Does your knee hurt? Perhaps you're stopping yourself from going forward in life. You can find many mind connections to body ailments in *You Can Heal Your Life* by Louise Hay. In his book, *Healing Back Pain: The Mind-Body Connection*, John E. Sarno talks about the link between low back pain and financial or other worries.

The impact that the mind has on physical health is becoming better understood. Endorphins in the brain cause euphoria and pain relief, and in the immune system, endorphins bolster our health. Grief, depression, fear and panic actually suppress immune function, while laughter, love, faith and self-acceptance stimulate a positive immune response. With a suppressed immune system, we can get sick more often. Our weakest areas will become vulnerable. We want a healthy immune system to protect us from bacteria, cancer cells and other unwanted invaders.

Stress is an inside job. All of us have a running commentary going on in our minds regarding thoughts that result from our past programming or belief systems. Past programming comes from parents, siblings and teachers. Our own experiences and outlook on life also play a large part.

Some of those commentaries going on in our heads are positive and some are negative. Negative self-talk isn't all bad. Your good sense could be warning you: "If you take one more drink, you'll be in trouble" or "Don't touch the stove; you'll get burned." Our survival mechanism depends upon such types of internal alerts.

Nonetheless, if you continually put yourself down, the effect becomes part of the stress problem. Those who also see the world in unreasonable or irrational ways cause themselves a lot of stress. Self-confidence plunges. We need a boosted self-confidence for many instances in life: finishing a project, making a presentation, dealing with our spouse's parents, driving in heavy highway traffic and more. Yes, it's stressful applying for a job; however, your body does not need to perform inner cartwheels!

Begin to view events as challenges instead of threats.

The Frazzled Woman's
3 Steps to Think Positively

If it were so easy to think positively, most women would. What can you do?

1. Notice Yourself Thinking Negatively

Thoughts become words. Notice when you are being a 'downer' by bombarding yourself with negative thoughts. Remember that thinking positively boosts your immune system. Positive thoughts and actions actually increase the amount of killer cells in your body. These natural killer cells fight off disease and bacteria. You will feel a whole lot better with positive thoughts than with negative ones.

Many people think negatively because of ingrained superstition. In their culture, someone may have told them that if one thinks too many good things, something bad will happen. These people spend their lives thinking negatively. Ironically, they subconsciously hope good will come out of it. Are you willing to discard old habits for brighter new ones? Yes? Then:

It's time to ditch the black cloud and look for the rainbow!

Some people imagine they're jinxed. If you have a fender bender, do you think, "I'll never learn to drive properly," or

"I'm a target: cars always run into me," or "I'm an idiot"? Does this person sound like the life of the party? Most people like to be around others who are cheerful and upbeat. There are enough dreadful things that happen in the world to bring us down. Don't be a doomsday prophet or a martyr. You won't get invited out.

When you repeat negative messages to yourself on a regular basis, it's self-defeating. You could set yourself up for a self-fulfilling prophecy.

Do you hate your body? Poor body image or body hate shouts out negativity and deflates a woman's self-esteem. In a Louis Reed Poll, 99% of women said they were dissatisfied with their features or figures. "I've got boulder thighs", "chicken legs", "flat chest", "oversized chest", "big nose", "too small a nose", "no hips", "too large hips". Women often set up an unattainable view of beauty and then berate themselves for not living up to it. In the process, one's outlook, enjoyment of life and immune system all get dragged down. When we feel negatively about appearance, our levels of stress increase.

2. Challenge Your Negative Self Talk

If you find yourself with a negative thought, "I'll never make it" or "I'm a fool," ask yourself, is this really true? Can you really be sure that you won't make it? Are you truly a fool…all the time? Surely you make a few good decisions! Our actions can usually be remedied. If you've made a mistake, hurt someone by what you've said, you may be able to rectify that wrongdoing, or at least apologize and somehow make reparations. Everyone makes mistakes. It's part of living. Each day is a new slate. Each moment is a new beginning.

Challenge your assumptions and beliefs. If you have to give a speech do you think, "I'll make mistakes, they'll laugh at me"? You need to challenge such thoughts. "Who says I'll make mistakes? Who says they'll laugh at me?" Start thinking "I will do very well because everyone is interested in what I will have to say." Then just give it all you've got. You cannot lose. Actually from my experience as a speaker, I've found that if you make a mistake, the audience sees you as human. Their empathy for you and their connection with you increases.

Mistakes are lessons to be learned.

If you are thinking negatively about a situation over which you have no control, get mobilized. Challenge the thought and then seek to change it by seeing it in a different light.

3. New Spin on Your Thoughts

Tune your internal radio to a positive station. Arm yourself with phrases that strengthen your self-confidence, your mood and immunity, such as:

- I am a worthy person.
- Look how far I have progressed and I'm still moving forward.
- I am not helpless.
- I can and will take necessary actions to pull through this difficult situation/event.
- I know I will be okay no matter what happens.
- I have beautiful eyes, skin, hair (or whatever you think is beautiful about your body).
- I'm dependable, honest, attractive, a hard worker (or whatever positive traits you feel you have).

Pick a positive phrase that is meaningful for you, or compose one. Post it (or several) near your computer or work station. Repeat them to yourself each day. They will bolster your confidence.

Now, write out one negative message you regularly tell yourself. Go through the three steps above to notice it, see if you can challenge it, and then apply a new spin to that one thought. In doing so, you will take charge of it.

Positive Stress and Feeling Challenged

Is there such a thing as positive stress? Feeling challenged or going forward in life (starting a new job or getting married, for example) can be described as positive stress. It's that excitement at little things: a beautiful sunset, finishing a crossword puzzle, attending your child's first school concert. It's the flutter of those little butterflies in your stomach when you're keen to try new things. Do you still feel passionate about life, about being here on this earth?

Yesterday I visited Kathy. Kathy is 46, a lovely petite woman with bright blue eyes. She goes to theater, to movies, takes swimming classes every morning and goes on outings every weekend to the country. Kathy is a paraplegic. She can see, hear and smile. She can move only two fingers and she speaks to people using those fingers on her little typewriter affixed to her wheelchair. Kathy likely won't live too much longer. She used to be a banker. She was married, but since her illness, divorced. In our last conversation on her keyboard, she plunked out: "I'm lucky. I have a good life." I was stunned.

She also said through her keyboard that she was worried about one of her caregivers who needed to lose some weight. Kathy requires nursing care 24 hours a day. She cannot eat anymore except by feeding tube. She smiles when you talk to her. She appears to get joy out of each moment and she still feels for others.

Now there's a lesson in perception of events. Certainly we can do at least a fraction of that.

Work through your emotions. So what have you got to complain about today? As a child, if I would excessively whine or complain, my mother would say, "Complaints on the fourth floor!"

I'm not saying that we have to pretend things are okay all the time. We need to get out our emotions and work through them instead of stuffing them deep down. Surely Kathy came face to face with her emotions and has worked through them. You can work through yours.

Examine your sadness, regrets, feelings of inadequacy, fears or anger at someone in your life. Reflection is a great place to start the healing process. It's never too late.

"The game ain't over 'til it's over."
—Yogi Berra, former catcher for the New York Yankees

Your Extreme Stressor

Right now, decide on one thing that causes you continual or extreme stress:

It may be your **fear** of flying.
It could be **anger** at your father or mother for not giving you what you expected.
It could be your **sadness** at losing a dear friend, parent or child.
It may be **regret** at not doing something.

Write it down in your journal. Write (or think) about how it bothers you. Keep writing or thinking until you can't write or think anymore. From your own insights, formulate an action plan, some steps you can take to go forward. If you're stuck and can't get through it, talk to a friend, clergyman or get some professional help. Remember step one: Do something!

A note from my own journal:
I am afraid of flying and must fly for my job.

I feel a lack of control when I'm on an airplane. I feel claustrophobic. For two weeks before I have to fly, I experience extreme anxiety. I can't sleep. I imagine plane crashes and feel in a state of panic when I am on the plane, especially if there is any turbulence.

If you share my fear of flying, your action plan may include one or more of the following:

- Get professional counselling. Learn ways to change old thought patterns.
- Examine the basis of your fear. Are you afraid your children will be left orphaned? Make a will and set up guardianship for the children.
- Afraid you haven't accomplished enough in your life yet? Figure out the steps you need to start accomplishing your goals.
- Take a Fear of Flying course that many airlines offer.
- Change jobs.

Note: Putting some of the above strategies into practice has helped ease my fears.

Carrying Anger

Donna, married and with two teenage children, harbored anger for her father Jim. He was a decent man, always worked hard, was faithful to her mother, and was not abusive. Jim loved a good joke and enjoyed talking to everyone he met. So what was the problem? He seldom talked to Donna. His interest in his children was nil. He left child rearing to his wife. Donna craved a conversation, a good word, a pat on the back, her dad showing up at a school function. It hardly happened. Jim seemed to live on another planet.

After her mother died, Donna became a part-time caregiver for her aging father. She experienced torrents of resentfulness. Jim's confinement to a wheelchair made him frustrated, lonely, and he exhibited the anger of a bull. He expected his daughter to attend to him. Donna's brother was nowhere in sight. She felt stressed, trapped and frustrated at playing the 'good daughter' while she had a family of her own to care for. Donna became the emotional whipping post for Jim's unfortunate situation.

Eventually Donna found a counsellor who could help. Examining her anger revealed another emotion that bubbled beneath the surface—grief. She grieved for the lost years of affection and the ache in her heart from her father's emotional absence. Once she faced her negative reactions, she realized she had to **let them go**. That was the trick. After all, she couldn't bring back the years.

She learned to confront her father's angry words with kind firmness. "Dad, I know this is difficult for you and I'm doing my best. Please do not yell at me." If he did yell or was unkind, she wouldn't show up the next day. When she returned, he was surprisingly more subdued and gentle.

Their new relationship gave her the freedom to embrace her dad's positive traits—his love of life and his enduring responsibility for his family. She grew happier when she changed her attitude and began to focus on the positives in her own life. Finally, she looked for ways to nurture herself and her family by finding respite services and alternate home care for her dad. Everybody won.

Donna had been playing the 'victim' role, believing everything was happening to her. She felt she had no control, but control was within reach all along, waiting for incentive. Gratitude replaced grieving and filled her heart for all that she had accomplished in her life. She even got to hear the words she had longed for. Before he died, Jim grasped his daughter's hand and said, "Donna, you know I've always loved you."

Donna resolved to be different with her own children and with other people. She would let them know that she loved them by showing them with her actions and words. By becoming more aware of her family, her friends, and doing the things she loved, she began to realize that **action** is much more productive than resentment. And it all started by simply setting enough limits to prevent burnout.

Don't become or stay a victim. If we don't act, we become victims. A victim mentality will ensure that you stay in one spot and never go forward. As a victim, your constant companions become depression, feelings of inadequacy, lack of self-esteem and a definite lack of energy. Life grips you in a steady struggle. It becomes **Stress with a capital S**.

Why do women stay in the victim mode? We may think that this approach ensures emotional safety. When we are victims, we can blame others. It's easier than taking responsibility for our feelings. It may be too painful to look at the reasons we fell into the victim mode; and thus, we can rationalize feeling sorry for ourselves.

Self-pity doesn't ask to examine the past. It simply shields its owner against change.

It's not easy to transform ingrained habits. Perhaps you witnessed victim behaviors in family members, making them seem a 'normal' response to problems. Some women may mistakenly think that feeling sorry for themselves is self-love. In reality, staying in the victim mode extends the length of our misery and prevents self-growth.

Notice if you are self-pitying. Ask yourself, "What is the benefit for me to stay stuck in this 'poor me' state?" Right now, put your right hand on your left shoulder and put your left hand on your right shoulder. Hug yourself. You're okay.

Take-Away Gems

1. Recognize your self talk. Is it mostly negative?
2. Ask yourself: Are these thoughts really true?
3. See events as challenges instead of threats.
4. Start to reinforce yourself with positive messages.
5. Examine your feelings. Know they can change.
6. Recognize the importance of an action plan to go forward.

You can transform pessimistic views into creative challenges that make you feel smart, effective and in control. After all, you deserve to feel happy; your mental and physical health depends on it.

CHAPTER THREE

Your Glass
Half Empty Or Half Full?

Perhaps you get up in the morning and think, "Oh God, another day!" An alternative thought could be, "Thank you God, another day!"

Are you a worrier? Do you become anxious if things don't go smoothly? Do changes in your life cause you extreme stress? Do you harbor a lot of anger or resentment?

Are most of your days spent in fear?

Where does all that stress come from? It comes from within, from our belief systems. Stress arises from letting our thoughts or emotions go wild and allowing the worst fears to surface. It also develops when we do not accept what is. If only we could find the joy in what we already have.

Sandra's glass is half empty. She has three grown daughters. Her two eldest daughters received scholarships to study at elite universities. They are brilliant and excel. The third daughter barely made it through high school and is now attending a local college. Sandra is devastated. She is ashamed to tell her friends. She can't sleep and worries that her youngest daughter will end up in a menial job.

It would help if Sandra could find a way to lower her expectations of her third daughter and start showing approval of her. Seeing the glass as half full would be demonstrated by being thankful her daughter is healthy and still wants to learn. Children, no matter what age, need to feel proud of themselves so that they can work to reach their potential. Parental approval goes a long way in boosting that self-esteem.

Sandra's sister, Jennifer, finds herself in very different circumstances. Jennifer has one son who has a mental illness that struck him at age 18. He has been in and out of hospitals. At 20, he is now stabilized and Jennifer is hopeful for his future whatever path he takes. He is in a program to help him go forward. Jennifer's glass is already half full, perhaps more, because she has a positive outlook on a difficult situation.

Worry = Stress = Worry

In any given situation, it's possible to imagine the worst that can happen. My husband maintains that 90% of what you worry about never happens. He's right! The words stress and worry are interchangeable; when we worry excessively, we think negatively. Our bodies go into the 'fight or flight' mode.

In the medieval era, 'worry' actually meant to choke or strangle. Have you ever walked the floor waiting for your teenager to come home? Have you ever lost your child in a large shopping mall? If so, I don't have to tell you about that strangled feeling. It's fear that something has gone very wrong. When it involves our kids, it's difficult to avoid. Mothering and its protective instincts open avenues of fear.

Thankfully, in most cases, teenagers come straggling through the door past their curfew, and missing children are found wandering in the mall. But it's the small minority of those who are not found that our minds dwell on. Why is it that we focus on the worst outcome right away? It's because our kids are so precious to us that we can become stalked by guilt. Perhaps we might turn our heads for a minute, the wrong minute. In the case of teenagers, maybe we remember our own teenage years and understand the attitude of immortality that young people feel. We recall our own risk-taking stunts, even though we lived to talk about them.

There is a positive side to worry: a little worry may keep you on your toes. An occasional worrier may take appropriate action. If you are overweight and you worry about your health, you can make an appointment to see a nutritional consultant or join a weight loss and exercise club. However, if you just worry and do nothing, your fears may become reality.

*"God grant me the serenity to accept the things
I cannot change; the courage to change the things
I can; and the wisdom to know the difference."*
— Bill W., Founder of Alcoholics Anonymous

Excessive worry becomes anxiety. Chronic worry is dangerous since it causes you to constantly imagine negative, undesirable events; you become anxious, stressed and exhausted. Worry can prey so heavily on the mind that it can even immobilize you. Before that happens, you'll need to take control of your thinking instead of letting it take control of you.

We think the mind is in control. It is not.
It's our will, our spirit, our good sense,
our determination—our higher self—that's in control.

People send me e-mails about all the terrible things that happen in the world. They caution me that there are people waiting to jump in my car and kidnap me. Sometimes they alert me about diseases and their warning signs, along with any number of terrible possibilities that can render me dead. I wonder if the people who send me those scary messages are so filled with their own fears that they simply have to share with someone.

Yes, we need to be street smart and to take care of ourselves. We need to be pro-active by feeding our bodies and exercising to ward off a build-up of stress chemicals. But we DO NOT need to live in fear.

It's all about quality of life, not longevity.

Living in fear produces stress and anxiety, which in turn upsets the immune system and you'll get sick more often. Don't listen to news stations all day; once is enough. When you listen to or watch news shows before bed, you set yourself up for a night of tossing and turning. Watch a funny TV show instead, or read or listen to some music.

Make time to socialize with friends. Go ice skating, bowling or dancing. Meet for dinner or invite friends to your place for a party. Make time for enjoyable activities and see how 'down-in-the-dumps' attitudes can disappear. Do what you can to get yourself out of negative, fear-based cycles. What helps me is spending fun times with my granddaughter. Reading stories, playing ball, singing songs, or having tea parties with her and her dolls always cheers me up, no matter what's on my mind. If you have a young child in your life – either your own, a relative's or neighbor's, taking the time to play (and revisit your own childhood), is a great stress reliever. Children love to laugh. By being in the company of a child and allowing yourself to enter into his or her joyful world, you'll banish fear and soothe your soul.

Panic: Escalated Fear

Consider the situation with the teenager who is 3 hours late coming home. Is your worry or stress controllable? It depends upon the circumstances. If you know where he or she went and can track down your adolescent, it's controllable. If not, you have two choices:

a) You can worry, think the worst and whip yourself into a state of panic.

b) You can feel concern, take some deep breaths and stay calm.

Many years ago I chose the panic response while my husband went back to sleep. He cares the same as I do for our children. So what was the difference?

He thought:
1. Our daughter's with friends. She lost track of the time.
2. She'll be home soon.
3. There's nothing I can do anyway, so I might as well stay calm.

Actually, my frenzy made matters worse. When the alarm clock read 2:30 a.m., and our daughter's room was still empty, I bolted out of bed, snatched up my husband's car keys and began driving madly around the neighborhood. My daughter had my car, and I knew she was with friends. Likely she wasn't far from home. I would find her. Well, I did.

There was my car, parked outside one of her friend's houses. I breathed a sigh of relief, but then I got angry that she had disregarded **our** rules of **her curfew with my vehicle!** Hastily, I scribbled an irate message on a scrap of paper and left it on my car window under the windshield wiper. I didn't want to knock on the door and make a scene, but I did want my teenager to know how upset I was with her.

Unfortunately, at that moment she emerged from her friend's house and was mortified to find her mother standing at the curb dressed in a housecoat and slippers. After a short, heated exchange of words, we retreated to the cars and pulled away. As I did, I checked my rearview mirror just in time to see her reach out of the driver's side window to fetch the note that I had left on the windshield. To my horror, the distraction caused her to plow the car into a pole.

The details bear the weight of a parent's worst nightmare: the car totaled; the arrival of an ambulance, police cars, and a frightening trip to the hospital. My unassuming husband's sleep was disturbed by a jangling phone and frightened wife.

My worry, frenzy and panic had gone over the top. I imagined I was in control of the situation. But truly, I was out of control. Happily, I can say that somehow, by the grace of God, my daughter was okay. She was sent home, shaken but intact.

That night, I learned the hard way how extreme worry paired with extreme action can be dangerous to one's health (and others)!

Tips for Worriers:

1. Take a worry apart. Analyze it, dissect it. Separate what is illusion (your spin on the worry) and what is real. Get the facts. Use cool, rational thinking. Understand and dispel the illusion side of the situation: the reality remaining will be easier to handle.
2. Breathe deeply to prevent the stress response from escalating. If you have a rocking chair, use it. The motion is soothing and can relieve tension. Otherwise, just sit down, cross your arms over your chest and rock back and forth.
3. Give away your worries to a Higher Power. You can pray, or just ask that the Universe please take care of your worries for you (or those who you are worried about). You can ask for protection too.
4. Allow yourself a distraction. We can only think of one thing at a time. Do something instead of stewing: read, watch a movie, listen to music or turn on the television. I find that cleaning out a kitchen cupboard gets rid of built-up tension!
5. For those of you who are disciplined, plan a meeting, a specific time to deal with your worries.

Emotions in Motion

Emotions (both positive and negative) are part of us: love, joy, excitement, surprise, passion, envy, fear, jealousy, hate, resentment. By the age of two, children experience most human emotions. It's okay to feel emotions. We become more alive if we are passionate and feel them rather than block them. But we do ourselves harm if we allow the negatives such as fear to rule our hearts, minds and bodies. To let negative emotions run the show is harmful to our health.

Ask yourself some important questions:
What causes you fear?
Who do you resent?
Who or what are you angry at?
What regrets do you cling to?
Who are you jealous of?

For more information on feelings, check **Chapter 9, Relationships: All We Need is Love. . . and then some**

The Effects of Unresolved Fearful Emotions:

Anger: Welled-up anger increases cortisol, a stress chemical which can initiate some forms of illness. Often, anger is fuelled by hurt or a lack of control about some issue. You may be angry if your sister or brother doesn't invite you to a family party, but truly isn't there an underlying feeling of being hurt? Perhaps your business partner makes a decision about your business without checking with you. The decision causes a financial loss, thus your anger and perhaps that underlying feeling, a lack of control.

Resentfulness: Pain is a by-product of resentment. For example, you may resent your sister because when you were both children, she got more attention and achieved higher grades than you. You blame her and harbor ill feelings because you think your parents loved her more. The resentment remains firm in you, causing trouble in your mind and body such as headaches, backaches, guilt, and anger; it also prevents any meaningful relationship with your sister.

Indifference: We communicate indifference when we neglect to make contact with others, especially for holidays or family events. Indifference destroys relationships and invites loneliness, both to you and those who are close to you. People think that you don't care about them.

Regret: When you live in the past, always replaying what you could have/should have done, you miss out on the good things in your life right now. Regrets drag you down.

Worry: Fretting and worrying replace pleasant thoughts, even though it's all about what hasn't even happened yet...and might not.

Jealousy: Being envious breeds hate and wastes your time. Your attention is fixated on the perceived success of others while you either neglect your own needs or engage in something ridiculous and/or regrettable in order to compensate.

These fearful emotions cause great distress in our bodies including sore neck, sore shoulders, lower back pain, aching feet, or even irritable bowel syndrome. If we don't deal with fears, we start running in any direction to avoid our own thoughts. Ta da! The Frazzled Woman!

Stop. Think. Turn Anger into Positive Action.

Doing is better than stewing. You can get through it. Get help with these negative emotions. When you do, they will pass and you will be able to get on with your life in a happier vein. You may even be able to see the positive side of a negative situation.

- If you turn anger into positive action, you can even benefit those around you. For instance, if you don't like the way your child's school is being run, do something. Write a letter. Mobilize other parents. Join the parents' group in your child's school. They may need your input.
- If you're angry about your job, go back to school or create your own business. Become an entrepreneur.

- If you resent your husband's mother, find something about her you can appreciate or tolerate, and focus on that. If she continually puts you down, in private find a calm way to tell her not to do that. If it's an occasional remark, let it go.
- If anger wells up because someone doesn't like your creative ideas, don't dwell on it. Get the anger out of your body. Go for a brisk walk, take some deep breaths. Don't let it bring you down. Underneath anger is hurt. Get over it. Feelings change and change and change. An hour from now, you'll feel differently. Retain your confidence in your creative ideas. Someone else will love them.

Every major author has had his or her manuscript refused by many publishers until someone thought it was great. If salespeople felt hurt at every negative response from their customers, they'd never be able to sell.

Emotional growth is an important tool for re-shaping life's challenges.

Most people who give digs or try to make you feel small usually feel small themselves. Yes it will hurt; no one likes to be put down. But don't allow insensitive comments to hurt you forever. Let them go. Let them go. . .

Don't let every little hurt be a stake in your heart!

Change—the glass as half empty or half full.
- You lose your job. You're scared you won't get a new one. You sit inside your house and worry about your bills. Your glass is half empty.
- You look for a new job that you feel you will enjoy more

than the last, one that is more suited to your skills. This can be scary, yet exciting. Your glass is half (or three-quarters) full.

Do changes put you over the top? Many people thrive on change. Most hate it. Many people eat the same foods every day, take the same route to work or even stay in the same job for 35 years while others change jobs every five years. For many, routine is stability; for others, it's stagnation. It all depends on your perception.

Studies show that multiple changes in a person's life in a short period of time can cause stress overload. Simultaneously moving your office and your home will put you over the top. If you can plan life-altering changes—a move, leaving your job, having a baby—make sure you don't schedule all of them in the same month! You'll be very stressed!

Getting separated from your spouse, smashing up your car or having it stolen can put you into the flashing red light range. Some things we can plan. Some things we cannot. Life happens.

We can't plan ahead for deaths in the family, floods, power failures or computer crashes. When those things happen, our glass becomes half empty. Eventual acceptance of those difficult events and looking for the positives will ensure that our glass is half full.

Actually, the last massive power failure became a mini-vacation for me away from work and computers. It was fun eating by candlelight outside with neighbors. There was no laundry to do, no cooking to worry about, just a lot of laughing under the stars.

I notice when I'm intensely in the moment
enjoying myself, I can honestly say my glass is full.

Pause to remember or to add to your journal a time when you were able to feel the excitement at some change in your life. If your memory is blank, then what do you need to do now to initiate something in your life that is creative, fun or exciting, so that your glass will become at least half full? A good book I recommend on the subject of change is *Transitions, Making Sense of Life's Changes* by William Bridges.

Tough times make you tougher. Can you think of difficult times that made you stronger? A parent's sickness and/or death, a business that went bankrupt, or are you in business with a partner you dislike?

Some people thrive under pressure: deadlines, contests, writing exams, problems to solve. You learn you can pull though. You may never be a fully developed human being if you are never challenged.

Feeling challenged will guarantee that you will never have a boring life. Demanding situations can lead to positive accomplishments such as writing a book, starting a new and exciting job, getting married! For some, even getting divorced can bring the start of an enriched, new life.

Good mariners are not created by calm seas.

Because of life's challenges, our determination spurs us on to accomplish goals. A strong will helps us realize our potential, to reach for success, and to achieve personal growth.

But I Have a Hard Life!

Do you feel you have a good reason to feel stressed, depressed and victimized? Is this you? Do you really want to focus on the negative aspects of your life? I've met people who were abused or politically oppressed, even tortured. Some were survivors of death camps.

Some have had more than their share of troubles and we need to have compassion. Maybe you're like me who survived health challenges such as severe back problems, intestinal difficulties and even a pre-cancer situation. And like me, you may have helped your parents through difficult illnesses and subsequent deaths. No matter what, all of us need to free ourselves from the victim mentality.

When life gives you lemons, eat a plum!

Addicts recover. The strength that they dredge up from inside themselves makes them stronger. I know former addicts who became addiction counsellors.

Some folks physically handicapped by an accident learn to drive, ski, sail, and even take part in The Paralympic Games. Others learn to enjoy the positive aspects of their lives. You can recover and live a productive life even with mental illness. You may even teach others how to do it. I know someone who did. Many women who suffered abuse have become counsellors for abused women. My own health was poor in my 20's and 30's. I learned how to regain it and now, many years later, guide others in their own healing journeys.

I'm not saying all these things are achieved without great effort. Life isn't always easy, I know. But using your will, determination and pure spunk, you can start somewhere to regain a happier you. It's in you. You can do it!

Recognize positives in your life. Think positively. It is a great goal and a good first step. Write down the many positive aspects of your life. Think of nothing else but those affirmative, encouraging points. Read over the list from Chapter 2 about positive self-talk thoughts and what you are grateful for. Keep them posted, in view. Work to change your thought patterns.

Repeat to yourself: Each day in every way, I'm getting stronger and healthier.

I'm not saying that we can walk around in 'la la' land as if nothing ever bothers us.

Unpleasant events, rude people, bullies, sick relatives, world politics, extreme weather, and a host of other things will upset you. Just don't let it endlessly upset you. Remember, you can change your perceptions and not let your thoughts ruin your life.

To wallow in unhappiness will lead to depression, stagnation and greater stress.

If you are unhappy about something, this may not be a bad sign because the glass is still half full. Discontent inspires us to create something new. All artists, poets and authors, songwriters or policy makers know this. The best creative work comes from a feeling that 'something's not right.' The trick is to use this unhappiness as a springboard for greater achievements.

Get help if you're constantly depressed. If you find yourself feeling negative about everything, then you know it's time to make some changes. You may be suffering from clinical depression. If you think you are, it's a good idea to speak to your doctor. If you don't have one, go to a walk-in clinic. Often, depressed moods originate in physical problems in the body. Deficiencies in nutrients can also cause depression or anxiety. For more information, check **Chapter 7, This Is Your Brain Speaking: Feed Me, I'm Hungry.**

Take charge of your negative self-talk. Instead, use positive self-talk phrases to buoy your self-esteem. To ask a professional for help is another way for you to take charge of your negative self-talk. We limit ourselves when we speak negatively. Negative thoughts turn to negative words, turn to negative actions. Stop it somewhere.

Language of Limitation	Language of Results
There's nothing I can do.	Let's look at the possibilities.
I should have.	Next time, I will.
I can't.	I can or I choose not to.
I don't have the guts.	I have what it takes.
That's just the way I am.	I can choose a different approach.

Being Grateful

In your journal write a separate sheet entitled: **People and things I am grateful for.** Alternatively, sit back and ponder the topic of gratitude and where to place it in your life.

Recall the things you are grateful for. Here are some examples: I'm grateful I woke up this morning! I'm grateful that I can see, hear and have two arms, two legs. I'm grateful that I had a good dinner, that I have a job, or skills to find one. I'm grateful that I have shelter and food.

Include grateful thoughts for the people whom you love and those who love you. Think of the people who are important to you in your life. Think of those closest to you, perhaps family, friends, colleagues, and acquaintances. Feel the love, the warm glow, that tingling sensation; or in your mind's eye, see the smiles of those you love. Send them your love as well.

Have you ever received a phone call from a friend or relative you've been thinking about? Of course you have. Positive thoughts seem to travel through the air waves. Call someone you haven't spoken to for a while. You'll be glad you did.

Review this list every day and your attitude will change for the better.

Take-Away Gems

1. Worry: If you need to, get professional help with worry or anger.
2. Gratitude: Each day think of all the people that you are grateful for.
3. Challenges: Note challenges in your life that made you stronger.
4. Changes: Identify positive aspects of changes in your life.
5. Know that you can see the glass as half full and you will.
6. Make time for fun, joyful activities: dancing, singing, watching funny movies.

When you take these bold steps to take charge of your thoughts and emotions, your frazzled way of life will be on its way out.

Enough of basic surviving. Get ready for **thriving!**

CHAPTER FOUR

Relax, Relax.

Tips To Keep You Cool

You're too busy to be relaxed because, even when you try, you can't sit still. Your mind races, processing what has to be accomplished next. Perhaps you find that you walk fast, talk fast, eat fast and drive fast.

You finish other people's sentences for them because you think they are speaking too slowly. Your knee jiggles when you sit, your fingers drum the table or you have a twitch in your eye that comes at the oddest times. Accidents: you've had more than your share. If the pattern sounds familiar, no doubt you're frazzled! If anyone has ever asked you to take a deep breath, they've noticed your hyper state.

Count to ten. Relax. Calm down.

Frazzled living invites its companion, anger. You become explosive and easily enraged. You slam kitchen cupboards, yell and scream at those people closest to you—kids, parents, partner. Perhaps you're a tiger ready to pounce at the smallest provocation. You lose your cool when you see school books at the front door or wait for a salesperson that you think works too slowly. If someone makes a joke, you take it as a dig. You find you're developing road rage.

The foregoing symptoms point to a 'type A' personality, a term coined in the 50's by cardiologists Drs. Friedman and Roseman. Type A's are four times more likely to have heart attacks than the rest of the population. It used to be mainly men who demonstrated 'type A' traits. However, women's unprecedented entries into the workforce and added responsibilities have made them vulnerable as well. A woman's dilemma of wanting to please everybody (being an overnurturer) makes matters worse. Women's health is at risk and we need to do something about it.

Women who are 'type A's' have a heightened stress response a great deal of the time. Unfortunately, **they begin to think this is normal.** The stress response, a biological reaction to a stressor, is supposed to turn on when we need it. Then we can run faster and have added strength to fight if we need to. When the crisis has passed, the relaxation response in the body takes over to calm us as the body returns to homeostasis (normal functioning). It's like a switch in our body going on and off.

However, the Frazzled Woman's switch is turned to ON most of the time.

Your top five biological reactions to stress:
- Release of sugar into the bloodstream to create more energy to fight off the stressor
- Increased cholesterol in the blood to create energy and to take over when blood sugar levels drop off
- Reduction in sex hormones which results in decreased libido
- Release of thyroid hormone (thyroxine) to speed up the body's metabolism to burn fuel fast, giving strength to fight or flee
- Decreased digestive activity; energy goes to the limbs for survival

All of this is wonderful if you're being chased by a Bengal tiger. However, I haven't seen too many tigers wandering around the streets lately. A woman's stress response turns on if she finds herself late or in a traffic jam. It turns on if her kids won't listen to her, if her boss asks her to stay another two hours after closing time. The stress response becomes activated especially if she loses information in her computer or has an argument with her spouse!

The Frazzled Woman sets herself up for: high cholesterol, increased blood sugar, low sex drive, overactive or underactive thyroid, digestive problems, aches and pains, and insomnia. Her quality of life sinks.

Women need to cool their jets!

Stop the stress response in its tracks! I'm asking you to notice when you first feel the stress response in your body. Be aware of a pounding heart, sweaty palms, tense stomach, fast breathing, aching neck or a racing mind. They are signals of the stress chemicals surging through your body. You can put a stop to them and protect your health. You can control the outcome.

1. Be aware of the signals of the stress response!
2. Practice deep breathing techniques.

Relaxation techniques can take many forms. The top three are body-focused tension relief such as deep breathing, stretching and massage. Yoga, visualization and meditation are also mental techniques which can calm, center, or clarify the mind.

The goal of relaxation is to release unnecessary muscle tension as well as to quiet the mind and body. The mind and body work together in harmony to bring about relaxation. When we calm our cluttered minds, we slow down breathing and reduce tension. Physical relaxation, such as stretching or deep breathing will bring increased oxygen to the bloodstream. When we exhale, we increase the capacity to expel wastes and release tension. After all, breathing is our natural tension-releaser. We do it every living minute, awake or asleep.

Most people in the seminars I conduct greatly enjoy relaxation techniques. I repeatedly hear the comments: "Deep breathing is a life saver," "I can't believe the importance of just taking a deep breath," or "Thanks for helping me feel sane again."

Simple relaxation techniques help to immediately reduce stress levels. Some feel that when they access the relaxation state they touch their own spirituality.

Relaxation helps you to:
- Activate natural healing powers
- Allow yourself time to relax
- Be a better problem-solver
- Gain insight and tap into your inner wisdom
- Have more fun and ease throughout your day
- Increase creativity and well-being
- Set and reach goals

When a woman is happy, everybody is happy!

When I attended relaxation seminars, my mind and body became relaxed and calm. Just thinking about the sessions as I write this puts me into a slower mode. The more I practiced the breathing and other techniques, the more my mind stopped jumping around; the knots in my stomach dissolved; illnesses abated. My face took on a calmer expression. I felt more in control and at ease throughout my day.

Many medical conditions respond to relaxation. Do you have hypertension, chronic pain or cluster headaches? Then you will respond positively to yoga and deep breathing.

Are you a shallow breather? If you watch a baby lying on its back, its abdomen rises and falls with each breath. At this moment, does your belly expand and deflate as you breathe? Likely not. We tend to become shallow breathers as we age. Lack of oxygen in the lower part of our lungs only adds to the stress response. We don't think about our breathing too much. It's too bad we don't. Life depends on it.

Focus on your breathing. Right now, just notice your breath going in and out through your nose. Be aware how the air goes down into your lungs and out again. Do this for about a minute. Just focusing on your breath is a way of relaxing.

Time to Breathe

Stop now, and take a truly relaxing breath . . .
Inhale through your nose with a shallow breath . . .
And exhale through your mouth . . .
Inhale slightly more . . . and breathe out with a sound,
 perhaps a sigh . . .
Inhale more deeply . . . and exhale forcefully . . .
Inhale to capacity, as much as you can . . .
And breathe out completely, emptying your lungs all
 the way . . .
Repeat this breath cycle ten times . . .
Or until you feel completely relaxed . . .
Now, maintain a steady rhythm of breathing in and out.

The Wonderful Diaphragm

Singers can belt out a tune because breathing through the diaphragm gives power to their voices. They are mindful of breathing deeply to protect their voices, sing on key and hold notes. Speakers, singers—and especially women who often feel they have 'lost their voice'—can find it again with more attention to breathing. For all humans, breathing depends on a rhythmic contraction and relaxation of the diaphragm. The primary function of the respiratory system is to supply the blood with oxygen. Blood is your lifeline because it delivers life-giving oxygen to all parts of the body.

The diaphragm is a sheet of muscles that is located across the bottom of the chest cavity and just above your navel. It can be likened to a balloon or bellows. When the diaphragm contracts, oxygen is inhaled into the lungs. When the diaphragm relaxes, carbon dioxide is pumped out of the lungs. This exchange of gases is the respiratory system's means of getting oxygen to the blood.

When we deep breathe, we allow more oxygen to get to the blood. Getting those bellows working in top form also gives your brain a boost. Your brain needs 25% more oxygen than the rest of your body!

Let's learn to breathe more deeply. When your body is in the fight or flight mode, if you breathe deeply, the slow breathing action of your lungs against your fast beating heart will halt the stress response. All the toxic stress chemicals that cascade through the body will stop.

After one of my relaxation seminars,
a woman leaped out of her chair exclaiming,
"The aches in my neck and back are gone!"

The Frazzled Woman's Belly Breathing

A woman usually walks with her stomach sucked in. In our youth and beauty culture, a flat stomach is akin to godliness. Now's the time to let it all hang out! Nobody's looking!

Put one hand on your upper chest and one on your diaphragm, just above your navel or your belly. Take a slow, deep breath in through your nose. See if you can get your diaphragm to extend. (Stick out your belly when you breathe in!) The hand on your belly should move out. As you breathe out through your mouth, your lower hand goes back into its original place. Your upper hand on your chest should not move; just your lower hand on your diaphragm or belly should be rising and falling.

Try this a few times: Gently breathe in through your nose down to your belly and breathe out through your mouth. You already are giving your body (and brain) more oxygen. If you cannot get your diaphragm to move, try the exercise lying on your back. This way, you will be able to get your belly to rise and fall when you breathe deeply. Then try it again sitting upright.

The following is a short, ten second breathing break you can do at any time of the day. If you're driving, don't close your eyes! Just do the deep breathing part.

Ten Second Break

- Take a slow, deep belly breath. Count to 4 slowly as you inhale and exhale.
- Take a second deep belly breath. Close your eyes as you start to inhale.
- As you exhale, imagine or feel warmth coming over your body at your head and flowing into your hands and feet. Perhaps you can visualize warm sunshine or a heat lamp over you. Your body starts to feel heavy.
- As heaviness and warmth are flowing in, think or repeat the phrase "I Am Calm."
- Alternatively, you can also think "I Am" as you breathe in and "Calm" as you breathe out.

Repeat this exercises a few times and notice if you feel any calmer. Open your eyes.

For those visual people, another variation of this exercise is to breathe in and visualize waves from a deep-green ocean rolling onto a sandy beach. As you breathe out, see the waves recede back to the ocean. Repeat until you feel calm.

For those people who mostly respond to audio stimulation, listen so that you imagine that you hear the waves crashing to the shore. For those kinesthetic types who need to feel the water, imagine yourself sitting on a beach while the waves lap against your legs. Then feel the waves pull out to sea while the wind blows through your hair.

Count Your Breaths

This exercise is similar to Belly Breaths.

- Take a deep breath into your nose to the count of four. You can close your eyes.
- Hold the breath to the count of four.
- Breathe out to the count of five.
- Repeat a few times.

These exercises are not complicated. They can be repeated as many times as you need to during the day. If you come home from a day's work and feel exhausted, lie down and do a few Belly Breaths or Count Your Breaths. The state of relaxation can be deeper than sleep. You will be revived. When you play some quiet music, you double the relaxation experience.

"Music hath charms to soothe the savage breast,
to soften rocks, or bend a knotted oak."
— William Congreve, playwright

Music helps people think more evenly on both sides of their brains, increases cognitive skills, and boosts creativity. It touches our emotions, helps us feel, releases what's bothering us, and can even offer us hope for better times ahead. Listening to melodies helps us to let loose with feelings that may be causing distress. It inspires us to examine our lives. Music is a great stress reducer.

Musical Prescriptions

According to author Kate Mucci, a therapeutic musician, harpist, author and recording artist, music also has measurable physical effects on the body. Certain kinds of music actually lower blood pressure and heart rate, regulate breathing, and lower cholesterol.

Research has shown that soothing classical East Indian harp music and chant actually increase the body's ability to ward off disease.

People undergoing surgery require less anesthesia, awaken from anesthesia more quickly with fewer side effects, and mend more rapidly when healing music is played before, during and after the surgical procedure. Patients recovering from heart attacks and strokes respond much more quickly to treatment when soothing music is played in their rooms.

Many studies have shown the incredible effects that music has on chronic pain. It benefits patients suffering from back pain, fibromyalgia, chronic fatigue syndrome, and pain from injuries. Grief, loneliness, even anger are all better managed when appropriate music is added to therapy. Autistic children and children diagnosed with Attention Deficit Disorder all react positively to music therapy. Kids with learning disabilities show remarkable improvement in mathematics, reading and reasoning skills when they are exposed to appropriate music.

I recall giving a concert for children in a hospital; many were from the psychiatric ward. Most of the children were engaged, singing and clapping along. When I asked for volunteers from the audience to participate by playing rhythm instruments, a young boy at the back of the room immediately shot up his hand to be chosen. He came up to the stage area and was part of the make-shift band. He played the small drum enthusiastically, as though he had always played drums. Later, I was astonished to discover that that for the past six months, this child had been in a deep depression, not able to speak a word or respond to anyone. Music can heal.

Listen to soothing music that you love; your body and mind will respond favorably. To obtain some guided imagery CD's and other breathing exercises, check work by Eli Bay. Other CD's of great benefit are *Solitudes*, nature compositions by Dan Gibson and relaxation music by Hennie Bekker. Music by composer Ron Harrison also soothes the soul.

To trigger relaxation, it's best to do these types of calming exercises every day. You'll fall into a deeper sleep at night. The relaxation you gain during the exercises has been shown to be at an even greater depth than sleep itself. The challenge is to take the time to develop the skills. Even 10 to 15 minutes per day can make a big difference to reduce your overall stress levels.

Other Ways to Relax

Give yourself 'noodling' time every day. Women need down time—time with nothing scheduled. It doesn't mean you have to sit and do nothing. Frazzled Woman, you will always have good ideas about what to do. You just don't have to act on each one!

Wander around a museum or an art gallery. Read the newspaper. Rest or sleep. Plan. Do your nails. Clean out your sock drawer! Organize your week on paper. Soak in a tub. Take some time for you. It's amazing how you can work out problems in your mind during 'noodling' or down time.

Aaah . . . get a massage! If your body is in knots, there's no better way to release the tension than to get a professional massage. Many insurance plans offer coverage and the benefits are remarkable. Massage can assist healing by releasing lactic acid in the muscles.

Research in massage therapy has been ongoing for more than 120 years. The following are some reported benefits of massage:

At the University of Miami School of Medicine's Touch Research Institute, researchers have found that massage is helpful in decreasing blood pressure in people with hypertension, alleviating pain in migraine sufferers and improving alertness and performance in office workers.

An increasing number of research studies show massage reduces heart rate, lowers blood pressure, increases blood circulation and lymph flow, relaxes muscles, and improves range of motion. Although therapeutic massage does not increase muscle strength, it can stimulate weak inactive muscles, thus partially compensating for the lack of exercise and inactivity resulting from illness or injury.

Try it. You'll like it!

Soak in a tub. Soaking in a warm bath for about 20 minutes with a cup or two of Epsom salts is an effective means of making the magnesium your body needs readily available. Excess adrenaline and stress are believed to drain magnesium, a natural stress reliever, from the body. Magnesium is necessary for the body to bind adequate amounts of serotonin, a mood-elevating chemical within the brain that creates a feeling of well-being and relaxation. Helping the body to ease muscle pain and eliminate toxins are additional benefits of the Epsom salt soak.

Over-fatigue is Adrenal Fatigue

If you don't take some relaxation, 'noodling' or puttering time, you'll find yourself getting adrenal fatigue. Those adrenal glands on top of your kidneys are marvellous resources. During the stress response (fight or flight response), they pump energy in the form of adrenalin into your system if you feel in danger or are threatened. They give you that extra push when you need it during an emergency.

When you push your adrenal glands too hard, too long, you'll feel exhausted. Then everything becomes stressful. After menopause, the adrenal glands take over most of the hormonal production that your ovaries were once responsible for including the estrogen and progesterone output for the body. If your adrenals are burned out, you'll have a more difficult time in menopause.

Adrenal Fatigue is a condition of the body in which the adrenal glands are exhausted and unable to produce adequate hormones and steroidal compounds. Persons suffering from Adrenal Fatigue (such as the Frazzled Woman), often suffer from chronic fatigue, sleep disorders, trouble getting out of bed in the morning, depression symptoms, lack of endurance, and trouble handling stress.

Adrenal Fatigue is not typically caused by one source, but rather a host of lifestyle factors that contribute to this condition as a whole. There are many causative factors such as physical and emotional stress, poor diet, and lack of physical activity, significant use of stimulating compounds (caffeine, nicotine, and amphetamines), lack of adequate amounts of sleep, and not enough time to relax. Relaxation techniques can clearly help Adrenal Fatigue by restoring the body to homeostasis and facilitating the healing process.

Proper lifestyle changes and dietary changes also help the adrenal glands to repair themselves and return to proper functioning. **(See Chapters 6, 7 and 8 for information about exercise, sleep and super nutrition.)**

Mindfulness as a Relaxation Technique

Living in The Now (practising mindfulness) is the best gift you can give yourself and others around you. "Mindfulness is an ancient Buddhist practice which has profound relevance for our present-day lives. This relevance has nothing to do with Buddhism per se or with becoming a Buddhist, but it has everything to do with waking up and living in harmony with oneself and with the world. . . .most of all, it has to do with being in touch."[2]

Our racing minds govern us. Mostly, we live either in the past or future. We think about our mistakes and brood about what someone said to us. Often we become fixated with tomorrow's 'To Do' list. While it's important for us to plan for the future or to remember important events in our lives, our main task as human beings is to live each day and each moment the best we can. Otherwise, we bypass The Now.

The Now is the very moment that you're reading this. An hour ago is gone, the next hour (or minute) isn't here yet. All we have is The NOW. When we are out of The Now, the consequences are often accidents. We stub our toe or walk into poles. When we are out of The Now we fail to really connect with others. It's as though we are living on the surface. We race around or drag ourselves from chore to chore, our minds a million miles away. Often we function without depth of feeling or thankfulness. It's depth of feeling that gives us our joyfulness and passion for all our tasks. Our thankfulness gives us a feeling of loving to be alive and appreciation for the preciousness of life.

Every moment offers you the opportunity to fully engage, to really live—even if you merely stare at your computer monitor.

2. J. Kabat-Zinn, *Wherever you Go, There You Are*, Hyperion, 1st ed. 1994, p.3.

My eyes feast on the beauty of the picture on my screen-saver: a glorious, sunlit autumn day with a blazingly bright orange and yellow tree in the foreground. Behind it, similar trees arch along a winding path. I'm drawn in by its splendor, and want to walk into the scene. When I see a beautiful photo or take a nature walk, my life becomes interwoven with the surroundings. I am awed and inspired by the splendor of creation. The screen image invites me to question my own direction: Where am I going? Where will this lead **me**? What does **my** future hold?

Often it's a good idea to slow down and ask yourself these questions: Do I have something to look forward to? Am I satisfied and fulfilled with my work and my life? Are my relationships meaningful? Can I make them more rewarding? Do I feel joy about something?

We all feel overwhelmed at times if we're working too many hours or have numerous stressors in our lives. We need to replenish, to take time for ourselves. Plan for a mini-vacation during the day or, if possible, for a longer getaway. Breathe deeply, letting your mind and body relax. Find something that is beautiful: a picture, a flower, a laughing child or even something as ordinary as a screensaver. Really look at it, and allow it to touch your heart in some way. You never know where it may lead you.

The future is really a progression of NOW moments.

Being Aware Helps to Get into 'The Now'

- Notice your breathing. Practice the breathing techniques outlined in this chapter.

- How are you sitting? Are you slouching, are your shoulders rounded?
- Take note of your surroundings. Pick one item in your office or wherever you are right now and really notice it. It could be your ring or your mouse pad. Notice everything about it—its lines and design and color. Remember to breathe. This little exercise will bring you to The Now quickly.
- Quit multi-tasking. While women have been genetically programmed to tend to their young and do a multitude of other things simultaneously, the mind can truly only tackle one task at a time. It switches back and forth very quickly, but in actuality, it only focuses on ONE thing at a time. Talking on a cell phone, while trying to make a left hand turn and eating at the same time is not only mindless, it's also a dangerous habit to acquire.
- Live consciously. When you eat an apple, don't just wolf it down, but really taste its tartness. Notice its texture, chew it slowly and enjoy the flavor right down to the last bite. If you eat a piece of chocolate, savor its silky smooth feeling in your mouth and its sweet taste. Enjoy it completely.

That's what living in The Now means—getting the most out of every moment, even mundane tasks like washing dishes! Feel the warm water on your hands and enjoy the sensation.

Experiencing The Now is to truly hear others. Make a point of listening intently when others speak to you. Look them in the eye. Be interested in what they're saying. Don't shuffle papers. Be fully with that person. Conversely, notice how you feel when someone isn't listening to you. It hurts when others aren't interested in what you have to say. Our self-esteem can be diminished. Treat others as you would like to be treated.

When we live in The Now, we bypass fear. Fear lives in our anxiety about the future: "I'll lose my job; I'll get sick; I'll get lost; I'll never make it". Staying in The Now reduces fear. Even if it's an unpleasant moment that we're facing, we can accept what's happening. Then, if possible, act accordingly to change it. Realistic optimism sounds like this: "Whatever happens, I can handle it."

Ultimately, when you stay in The Now, it opens up a world of possibilities to you—a world of POSITIVE consequences. The Now will help you feel more in control, more centered and grounded. Be aware; set your intentions to live in The Now. When we continue to live with our minds a million miles away, often thinking about being somewhere else, we can hurt those we love and live out our lives without depth in our days, hours or moments.

Even if it's impossible be in The Now all the time, noticing how you're conducting your moments is important. Let go of negative scripts; live consciously. Accept what is and enjoy the peace of being in The Now.

Sam Lived in the Moment

Many years ago, I used to visit a nursing home. Each time I went there, an elderly gentleman with only one leg was usually stationed at the front door, sitting in his wheelchair. He had a friendly greeting for all who entered: "Hi! Welcome to the nursing home, my name is Sam." He shook hands with everyone. For those visiting sick relatives, it was a cheery welcome. He had been a menswear salesman his entire life and for each man that came into the nursing home Sam always guessed what size suit he wore. "Size 42 tall, right?" Of course, he was always right.

Now I'm sure it must have been distressing when Sam lost his leg and came to the nursing home two years afterwards. His second wife of eight years could not care for him at home any longer. Sam had already lost his first wife a few years earlier. When asked what kinds of things he used to do, he would say, "I loved going for long walks." At 86 years of age, Sam wanted a prosthesis, a new leg, so he could walk again.

Doctors said he could never handle it. But he fought for and eventually got his new leg. He had to undergo therapy and special instructions at a rehabilitation hospital. It was a celebration when Sam, grinning from ear, came walking through the door of the nursing home on two legs. Eventually, it became too difficult for him to manage, and the prosthesis sat in the corner of his room. But truly, it had been quite an accomplishment.

On the coldest of days, you could find Sam sitting outside in his chair. He would remark, "What a beautiful day. Oh, the air is so fresh! Look at the beautiful trees and bushes! Listen to those birds!" He had a joke for all the nurses who passed by. Sam lived about two years in the nursing home before passing away. That man taught me a lot about living in the moment, about putting aside your troubles for a while and being able to enjoy your day. Thanks, Dad.

Take-Away Gems

1. Be aware of signals of the stress response.
2. Notice your breathing. Use your breath to calm yourself.

3. Practice some form of deep breathing technique each day.
4. Give yourself 'noodling' time.
5. Get a massage. Soak in a warm bathtub with Epsom salts.
6. Practice mindfulness. Live in 'The Now.'

The future is really a progression of NOW moments.

All aboard, Frazzled Woman! I know you can make each day, each moment count. Take the next train from Surviving to Thriving—a much better destination.

CHAPTER FIVE

The Elusive Healthy Balance

In reality, your mind, body and spirit will not be balanced each and every day.

Overall, because many of us are not consciously aware of what's bothering us, it becomes difficult to strive towards a balanced existence. We have to get off the rollercoaster to reflect on what's missing, what's excessive, and what's already 'just right.'

To ease into that 'feel-good' zone where you can better analyze your situation, this chapter is dedicated to helping you test your energy in each of your adult roles: physical, social, vocational, environmental, financial, spiritual, emotional and intellectual.

YOU are the engine that runs your life. If you lose yourself in the whole picture, everyone and everything else in your path suffers.

> *A healthy balance is all about managing energy.*

How well do you manage your pace? Energy is all around us. Our lives are exchanges of energy. We receive energy from the universe, from the sun, from nature that surrounds us. We receive oxygen from the air and breathe out carbon dioxide. Trees and other vegetation take in carbon dioxide and then expel it back into the environment as oxygen. So breathe in; you're feeding the trees and they are in turn feeding you!

We obtain energy from those around us through our relationships. Great ideas from others also give us energy along with physical activity, the food we eat and the water we drink. The more energy we receive, the more vital we become. We also give energy to those around us and to our work or other commitments.

The trick for the Frazzled Woman is to keep enough 'oomph' for herself.

A Wellness Wheel for You

All of us function in the many capacities that you see sectioned on the wheel on the next page. Probably you can think of a few more segments you could add to your wheel. Yes, we have a lot to contend with each and every day. It's easy to get out of balance if we're not vigilant.

The ignition key to getting the balanced engine started is self awareness. Let's work on self awareness first to get that key in hand. This next self assessment exercise will give you answers to guide you in that quest.

Each supporting facet of your life is shown as a spoke on a wheel, but that entire wheel must be cushioned by a band of self-love and self-responsibility.

When we love ourselves, everything works better. When we take responsibility for all our worlds, we are present and active participants in what happens to us. When we become responsible, we can leave behind attitudes such as: "I lost my job, how did that happen?" "I hate my apartment, what a dump—how did I end up here," or "I can't figure out why I weigh so much, I hardly eat anything."

Is self-love selfishness? Self-love is not to be confused with selfishness. Those who are selfish are mostly concerned with their own personal pleasure or profit at the expense of consideration for others. From my viewpoint, Frazzled Women try to do too much for too many. Self-love is having compassion for yourself, perhaps being able to laugh at yourself without self put-downs. Self-love is accepting yourself for who you are at this moment, **without guilt**. This perception may represent a change of attitude for you and, if so, it will take some positive self-talk messages to achieve it.

The Spokes of Your Wheel

Physical: I'm your body; please don't ignore me! Your physical spoke represents your body and its state, your nutrition, your activity level, and whether you sleep well.

During wellness seminars that I give, the majority of participants remark that this spoke of their wheel is the one that needs the most work. Many people are very body-aware while others don't even notice their bodies. We need to notice them. It's the only body we're going to get.

I'll always remember an exercise that my grade 2 teacher gave our class. We were asked to look in a full length mirror and carefully study our reflection in every detail. Then our next task was to draw a picture of how we saw ourselves in the mirror. We created a self-portrait with crayons. I don't remember having noticed myself in such an intense way before. Our pictures, with our names underneath, were displayed on the walls of our classroom. I loved seeing myself up there, wearing my favorite blue dress and grinning happily. I felt special and proud. Some people never take the time for a loving self-portrait, or an appreciative glance in the mirror. Do you? Chapters 6, 7 and 8 give detailed information on how to enhance the physical spoke of your wellness wheel.

Relationships: The essence of life. Your social/relationships spoke represents your family and your social life with friends, co-workers and acquaintances and how well you relate to them.

Some friends come into our lives for a season, some for a lifetime. Some may be messengers, introducing you to your life partner or teaching you something you need to learn. Sometimes we drift in separate directions from our friends as our values may change or we feel unsupported by them. Frazzled Women often unintentionally neglect their friends, even those whom they truly cherish. Their busy days have little room and perhaps they've lost touch and are longing to re-connect.

Women who are mothers are universally occupied with their children's physical and emotional needs. Children themselves will remind mother of her time-sharing limits with outside interests when they feel neglected. I can recall being home with my youngsters those first few years, often very involved with housekeeping and talking on the phone a lot because it was my lifeline to other adults. Then one day my toddler begged, "Mommy, get off the phone!" I knew then that I needed to spend more time stoking the mother-child relationship. I even wrote a song with that very title and later started a career singing for children. That song about mommy on the phone was my biggest hit! Why? It struck a nerve in both children and their mothers.

To be fair, I added a chorus for daddies: "Mommy, (or daddy) you've got so much to say, mommy, can't it wait for another day? I am just so tired of waiting all alone ... please mommy, get off the phone!" This song is from The Jim & Rosalie album Listen to Me that was Juno nominated for Best Children's Album in 1981.

Speaking of daddies or partners, with today's women having so many roles, primary relationships often suffer. While good communication is the cornerstone of relationships, sometimes we say too much and make matters worse. To listen is an important component of good communication not only with partners but also with others.

Tips to acquire the listening habit:
- Remember what someone is saying to you.
- Show respect for others' feelings.

- Be responsive to their ideas and thoughts.
- Have empathy.
- Be attentive. Maintain eye contact.

Remember that there is verbal and non-verbal communication. The non-verbal kind includes listening, nodding in agreement or other gestures. Touching our loved ones is a quick entry point to better relationships. The road back can start with a simple gesture of holding your loved one's hand, giving a hug, and spending more time with your partner.

That person may be missing you. Check chapter 10 for more information on enhancing relationships.

Vocational: It's just a job . . . or is it? Would you quit your job if you won a lottery? The vocational spoke on your wheel represents how you feel about your work whether it's in the home, outside the home or both. Know that there are mundane parts to every job—even if you love what you do. If you're an enthusiastic sales person on the road, you may dislike the paper work that goes with it. But nothing is perfect. If you are home with children, not every moment is filled with perfection. Diapers must be changed, meals need to be prepared, and homework often requires supervision. But truly, all work is being in service to others and is meaningful.

"There are three purposes of human work: 1) to provide necessary and useful goods and services to others; 2) to use and perfect our gifts (talents) that have been given to us; 3) to work in cooperation with others (teamwork) in order to liberate ourselves from inborn egocentricity. Truly, work is central to all human life."[3]

3.   E.F. Schumacher, P.N. Gillingham, *Good Work*, Harper & Row Publishing, 1974, pgs. 3, 4

> *Plain and simple, balancing the Vocational and*
> *Social/Relationship spokes is a definite*
> *challenge for working women with children.*

When I was eight years old, feverish, itchy and uncomfortable with chicken pox, my mother was compelled to leave me in the care of a neighbor while she went to work. Several times she got as far as the sidewalk and turned back to soothe my tears and sense of abandonment. I'm sure her day was heavy with anxiety, wishing she didn't have to leave me. These are the realities of the working mother and no matter whether you have a nanny, your mother, your spouse or a qualified babysitter at home, it's still wrenching to leave your child in alternate care.

Even with well-structured daycare facilities, working parents of young children often feel pulled in two directions. On one hand, your child is ill; on the other, you are expected at a crucial meeting in a client's office, perhaps out of town. Having reliable child care and even back-up, set up in advance, is essential to your peace of mind.

When I grew to adulthood, I was excited and involved with my music career, having worked as an instructor for children's music programs in libraries, nursery schools and day camps for many years. Finally, I had found a way to enter the professional recording world. However, that meant touring—sometimes being on the road for a couple of weeks at a time. The very things I had wished for had come true, yet I was tormented by having to leave my own children at home while I entertained others. The dream career became a nightmare. My health suffered.

When work and family are not in harmony, neither are women.

Compromises sometimes have to be made until children are older. Some women manage fine with working from the time their children are infants; others do not. Each person has to be clear about her own situation; examine it and decide if it's working or not.

Many women long to have a different job or career. Do you secretly wish that you could be a _____? You fill in the blank. Maybe you have thoughts about being an X-ray technician, a teacher, a business owner or landscape designer. If you decide to work on the vocational spoke of your wheel, be honest with yourself. Often, by simply acknowledging what you want (if it's feasible at the time for you and your family), you can then take the steps to find out how to achieve your goal, whether it's a pay raise, a promotion or a career change.

Volunteerism is also work. If you are actively engaged in volunteer work and you put in the number of hours as if it were a paid job, it may be time to decide if it's time to pull back. However, if the charity you are involved with is your passion, your reason for being and it doesn't interfere with other aspects of your life, then enjoy! However, if you really need to be paid for your work, you may not be able to volunteer 40 hours a week. Again life choices are up to you.

Environmental: Please save my planet. Your environmental spoke refers to your surroundings. Consider where you live, the neighborhood, and your place of residence.

Your neighborhood may be becoming noisier, dirtier, more congested with traffic or pose a danger for walking at night. These conditions may have developed gradually, and you have adapted, but it may be playing on your sense of pride. If your surroundings have allowed you to become disassociated from nature, you can do something about it, even on a small scale. If you see trash outside your home and neighborhood, do you pick it up?

Look objectively at your indoor space, both at home and at work. Bring in a healthy plant or two. Even small changes can transform plain surroundings to the attractive settings you see in magazines. Simple touches such as a vase with flowers or a small rug can bring an inviting, pretty atmosphere. Place some attractively framed pictures of loved ones or pets on your desk at work.

Get to a green space as often as possible and look around. Make a point of going for walks near trees, gardens and plants. Watch a brilliant, colorful sunset in all its glory or get up early to view a magnificent sunrise. Listen to birds sing their cheerful songs. Feel the sun warm your body; it will give you much needed vitamin D! Being in nature is calming and can make you feel whole again.

Try your best to recycle, use public transit or use your bicycle more often. 'Green' is the way to go today to save our planet for our children and future generations. Your health is intimately connected with the air, water and soil that surround you.

Financial: I hate being broke. Your financial world can be a sore spot. Everyone wants to make 30% more than they do right now, and everyone becomes jittery when the markets tumble. We feel vulnerable.

What is important is learning how to handle money in order to make it work in your best interests. While some fritter away income by overuse of credit cards, others live frugally, never enjoying a spending moment. Those are extremes. If you save and invest wisely along with spending appropriately for your income, there is nothing to feel guilty about!

From my experience, a lot of women (myself included) like to shop. Shopping along with chocolate can be stress relievers if not taken to excess. Otherwise, overspending and overeating become overstress!

Shopping and Chocolate. What else is there? Buyers' regret.

You may have a 'shopping gremlin' that's pushing you too far. If shopping reduces stress for you, yet you've already overspent, you may wish to reconsider your options. Instead of shopping for big ticket items, you can buy something small—a pair of socks, a pretty hair clip or a new lipstick. There's something about purchasing a new item that can raise a woman's spirits for a little while. It seems to renew her in some way, especially if she gets the item on sale! What a coup! However, shopping can become an addiction.

If you feel you must shop and your budget is gone, leave your credit cards at home! I know this may seem like letting the air out of your tires, but with credit cards, eager and ready to sacrifice themselves at every department store, restraint is often too difficult! 'Out of sight, out of mind' works for me. Either shop with cash that you have or just forget your visits to favorite stores for a while.

We all know that browsing leads to purchasing more stuff. In turn, more stuff can lead to devising devious ways of getting the bags into your home! Been there, done that. It's better to confront the 'shopping gremlin' once and for all. You may need to find a more productive pastime. It may be cheaper and healthier for you and your pocketbook to join a fitness club or take up a new sport or a hobby.

Women, with their huge purchasing power, are responsible for 87% of expenditures in North America. Yes it's true that men are hunters and women are gatherers. **Sometimes we gather too much.** How much 'stuff' do each of us really need for happiness? How much interest do we have to pay out before we 'get it'?

Money, or lack of it, creates many different attitudes: power or failure, pride or shame, freedom or enslavement. If you have more money than others in your family, you could feel misplaced guilt. If you have less, self-esteem can sag.

Some families have wealthy misers, some have careless spendthrifts, and some have generous, helpful types who can see their loved ones through a crisis. However, the best scenario is to seek self-reliance through financial knowledge and common sense.

There are 3 things you can do with money: spend it, save it, or donate it. If you need to moderate any of your money habits, there are excellent resources waiting on bookshelves and wonderful advisors at your bank branch or other investment counselors to help you sort out a plan. This financial restructuring is especially important when faced with looming recessions.

Not many escape some kind of economic hardship throughout a lifetime. However, when stock markets fall and there is talk of recession (which of late seems to occur every 10 – 12 years), it's difficult to live under the stress of financial doom. For those unfortunate people who lose their jobs or get laid off for a period, it's a scary time. I can only imagine what hardships my parents had to endure during the depression years of the late 20's and early 30's, when my mother stuffed her worn-out shoes with newspapers. In those difficult times, that was the only alternative to either buying new shoes or getting them repaired. But somehow my parents found jobs, relied on family for emotional and often financial support and rallied.

What can we do when faced with income and investment crises? To constantly worry doesn't help matters; it only paralyzes action. Remedies during economic hard times include tightening our belts (shopping for items on sale), and looking for innovative ways to make income. Socializing with friends at each other's homes with pot luck dinners, and cooking more instead of eating in restaurants are obvious ways to cut back (and still enjoy life). Some other coping mechanisms include giving up a second car, (or your only car, if possible). Others move to a city or town that has cheaper rent or property values, or take odd jobs to get them over the hump. Many cash in investments for a short time until the employment climate improves. Some take the time to get retrained especially if their former job is one that is disappearing due to technology. Choose your strategies; or if you are still uncertain, brainstorm the topic with close friends or relatives. There's always an answer.

Spiritual: There's a little star shining on you. Is your spiritual life active or inactive? For many, spirituality signifies belonging to an organized religion. However, a spiritual life can also be acquired by belief in some Force greater than yourself. Spirituality can mean believing in a soul, or spirit, or the power of prayer. A spiritual life could represent your meaning and purpose in this world. If you ask yourself: "Why am I here on this earth? What is it that I must accomplish?" then that too is spiritual. And so is helping others.

Having hope is spiritual. Do you feel alone or do you feel protected? The majority of people who have some spiritual connection are generally healthier than those who do not. If you are so inclined, go to a religious service. Read some books on spirituality, your own religion or others. I particularly enjoyed reading and learning about angels that surround us. Pray. It can bring comfort and many believe it can raise the possibility of healing.

Like a snowflake, you are unique. There's no one quite like you in this entire universe—even if you have an identical twin. You are not just one of the hordes of many living day by day. Your life has meaning and you can make it even more meaningful.

Intellectual: My brain is mush. Your intellectual spoke on your Wellness Wheel includes learning and growing. Are you complacent or inquiring? So where is your brain these days? You don't have to feel like an unsharpened pencil.

Tips to strengthen your intellectual spoke:
- Take time to read books, magazines or newspapers.
- Find an interesting item in the media that you can debate with friends.
- Listen to CD's on subjects that interest you.
- Watch the Learning or Discovery channels on TV.

Not surprisingly, your intellectual spoke can impact your relationship and vocational spokes. Keep learning and you likely will get a promotion, or you will be able to take on another vocation you will enjoy. In addition, your social life could improve—you'll have so much more to talk about!

Emotional: I want to scream! Ah . . . the emotional spoke of your wheel. Many women live their lives ruled by the emotions that reside in every spoke of their wheels. Our brains have a limbic system that governs feelings. How often do you rage, cry, scream, feel deeply, love, hate, fear? Are you in charge or without direction?

Jenny was prone to yelling. Her anger was always simmering at the edge of all her interactions. A small irritation to someone else could set off a tirade in her. When finally she decided to work on getting her emotions under control, she realized that she could get her points and feelings across without becoming loud and irrational. She now enjoys improved relationships at work and home. Being on overload can magnify small challenges. See Chapter 10 for more details about emotions and how they affect us.

No area of life stands alone.

Each spoke is dependent on the others for an overall smoother ride in life. For example, if your emotional world is out of control, you may not perform well in your vocational life. The mind and body connection underscores that emotions affect energy and physical health.

If you eat poorly, your energy levels could be low. Low energy could affect your productivity or the quality of your work, or your relationships. If you feel at a low in your spiritual world, you may have given up hope or feel that your life has no meaning. **Hopelessness can affect every other spoke on the wheel.**

How to Assess Your Own Personal Wheel

Using a pencil, place a dot on each spoke of the wheel that currently represents your situation (from 1 at the center, which is the lowest score—to 100 at the outer edge, which is the optimum score for you). Now, connect the dots, just as you did as a child in those puzzle books. What shape is your wheel?

If one or more of the spokes is in need of repair, your wheel will be wobbly. You may be experiencing a bumpy ride in life.

How do you feel about your findings?
Are you surprised?

Action steps:

- What improvements, if any, would you like to make in your Wellness Wheel profile?
- List two or three immediate action steps you could take to round out your Wheel.

When you feel ready, work on any spoke of your Wellness Wheel—preferably the one that seems most urgent. Changes take time; however, writing down your thoughts or thinking about making changes is a great way to begin. Finally, for success, turn thoughts into action.

But . . . I have no time for this! Living fully takes time and effort. Now that you've dropped some of your commitments, you'll have more time to consider how you got to be the Frazzled Woman. Your pathway out will depend on your approach. You don't have to do everything now. You could carve out some time in the next month or when your schedule will allow it. Just make sure you make a pact with yourself to start.

Write in your journal the date you charted your Wellness Wheel and your reactions. To keep your momentum and determination, also jot down a date when you can begin to re-align your wheel, one spoke at a time.

Personal self-growth is ongoing each day of your life. Every experience, every interaction affects your consciousness. Each day is a new slate. While each day brings some form of change, most humans resist it.

*To transform from surviving to thriving,
something's got to give! That something is CHANGE.*

Take-Away Gems

1. Keep enough energy for yourself.
2. Consider self-love as compassion for yourself.
3. Assess desired improvements to your Personal Wellness Wheel.
4. Take two or three immediate action steps to get you started.
5. Discuss your Vocational spoke of your Wellness Wheel with your family.
6. Recognize that willingness is the key ingredient to change.

By assessing your wellness quotient and making some tentative plans, you have already started some forward motion. Embrace your new self awareness with a determination to make lasting changes.

The Frazzled Woman is not really you.

On The Threshold

Filled with light, I stand
On the verge of something new,
My mind humming with excitement!
With outstretched arms, I long to
Soar like an eagle through space
And glide forward into time
To greet my future.
But I quiver like a child,
Feet firmly planted
In dark, familiar earth,
Afraid to plunge from the cliff,
Paralyzed, unwilling to burst
Through the fear of change
That will take me to plateaus
Of growth I so desire.

A gust of wind catches my dreams and hopes
Swirling them into colors
And like hot air balloons,
They float into azure blue sky.

"Wait for me! Don't go without me!"
I want to abandon fear, drop it like a stone
Into the murky sea below.
A balloon nudges, and invites me to soar
To new realms, when suddenly
I jump on, clinging for dear life
To ropes of possibilities.
Thirsty for change, I drink in the anticipation
Of tomorrows yet to be unfolded,
Abandoning my safe, warm place
For an unknown freedom.

by Rosalie Moscoe

CHAPTER SIX

The Health Trio
to Buffer Stress

1. Get off the couch
2. Get some shut-eye
3. You are what you eat!

"Someone's got to love my body!"

Some people don't even notice their bodies. That's Elizabeth, very intellectual. Elizabeth and many other Frazzled Women dash around oblivious to being 'body smart.' They don't notice when they are overweight or underweight, nor do they make the connection between the food they eat and their poor digestion. Most Frazzled Women have trouble losing weight since an overproduction of stress stores ready fat around the liver for the body to use as a source of fuel for the 'fight or flight' response.

On the flip side, there are stressed women like Elizabeth who are very thin and cannot seem to **gain** weight! Elizabeth never exercises as she hates sweating, which is to be avoided at all costs. It ruins her make-up, hair, and besides, she would have no time to rush home to shower after working out. She assumes she gets enough exercise being busy during the day. However, Elizabeth drives to work, sits at a desk for most of the day, and is actually quite sedentary, except for going to the shopping mall on the weekends (which she's sure counts as exercise).

She often works at her computer well into the evening and sometimes gets up later in the middle of the night to finish some work that is on her mind. Most days she feels tired, well beyond her 38 years. The circles and puffiness under her eyes seem to be getting darker and larger.

Elizabeth forgets her lunch and skips meals, often substituting a bowl of canned soup or a sandwich for dinner. Her weight keeps plummeting. She has no taste for food. (Actually she may be low in zinc, a mineral which affects appetite.) She feels that the problem must be her fast metabolism. She has no muscle strength, but for the most part she likes being thin. She thinks you can never be too thin or too rich. However, lately she finds her wardrobe hangs on her and she is very depressed about it. She avoids her mirror.

Her stress levels (and moods) are out of control. She's jumpy, often anxious and snaps at friends and family members. A permanent 'knot' resides in her stomach—a dull ache that won't go away. Elizabeth's left eye started to twitch last week and when she sits at her desk her knee won't stop jiggling. She feels that her boss is unfair to her and that her co-workers are ignoring her because they don't include her in discussions. She wishes she could pack her bags and leave town for a permanent vacation!

Elizabeth is not alone in her thoughts, feelings, body sensations and habits. Many Frazzled Women share the same kind of lifestyle which can lead to poor nutritional status, and stress-related symptoms. To their dismay, while many women eat more when stressed and pack on pounds, others, like Elizabeth, seem to lose their appetite and their weight falls to precarious levels. Our perception of events, our metabolism and how our bodies respond to stress is very individual.

You may have to step outside the safety of your routine. If you want to start somewhere to make some changes, there's no better 'bolt-out-of-the gate' strategy than to love your body. Yours is the only body you're going to get; you might as well take care of it. The first thing to do is notice it's there. A lot of women, like Elizabeth, just blithely continue their patterns and pay no attention to bodily messages: tender stomach, low back pain, aching shoulders, clenched jaw, headaches, exhausting monthly periods.

If this is you, you may be lucky. Your negative bodily sensations may be your body's way of giving you important messages. It's screaming at you, warning you to do something! "Don't ignore me!" "Pay attention to me!" "Take care of me." "Love me."

A Journey toward Loving Self Care: The Health Trio

1. Get off the couch (physical activity).
2. Get some shut-eye (adequate sleep and rest)
3. You are what you eat (so eat well!)

Quit thinking of these activities as ponderous chores that you **have** to do, and instead embark on a healthy lifestyle by nurturing yourself because you **want** to do so. That small shift in attitude may be the start of a new way of living. If you are already making headway using some of these stress buffers, congratulations and keep it up!

For those of you who may be thinking, "Cut it out. Who could want to exercise?" you may have to change the word exercise to 'physical activity,' 'moving your body,' 'getting active.' Exercise doesn't have to be boring or onerous. It can be a fun challenge.

Technology has deluded us into the belief that inactivity is a normal way to live.

PART ONE of the Health Trio: Get off the couch

You may wonder why you really need physical activity. The following are some reasons cited by Health Canada and other fitness experts.

Physical activity:

- Reduces stress, which in turn reduces toxic levels of cortisol and other stress hormones. You won't feel so frazzled.

- Helps relieve symptoms of asthma, improves your mood, and benefits your cardiovascular system. You will gain strength and a feeling of control.
- Lifts depression, reduces the risk of colon cancer, and helps normalize insulin levels. Moods will improve along with the possibility of better health.
- Improves your back and your bones and helps reduce the risk of osteoporosis. Aches and pains will subside (if you exercise according to your ability and progress).
- Increases the production of endorphins and reduces chronic pain. What Frazzled Woman wouldn't want this?
- Generates clearer thinking—a benefit when making decisions as well as meeting busy schedules.
- Accelerates your metabolic rate by stimulating the activity of your thyroid gland. Low functioning of a woman's thyroid gland can prevent weight loss.
- Builds muscle which makes your body burn calories more efficiently and reduces the risk of obesity. Burn those calories!
- Assists in controlling diabetes and menstrual cycles. There is a diabetes epidemic in North America, and Frazzled Women often endure debilitating menstrual periods.

Bonus: Exercise can also make you look years younger!

Some of you reading this may already be engaging in physical activity at a gym, or bike riding, going for walks, playing tennis or enjoying aqua-fitness programs. If so, keep it up and also remember the importance of the other parts of the Health Trio: sleep and nutrition. I've noticed many women who over-exercise and think that this is the only way to reduce stress. Yet many do not get enough sleep or eat a high quality diet and cannot figure out why they look and feel terrible.

Research shows that over-exercising combined with a low quality diet can slow down your metabolism and lead to stress fractures or tendonitis. Some women who over-exercise face irregular menstruation and a host of other related problems. Too much exercise can slow down your thyroid activity and the very goal of better energy will be thwarted, as you may feel exhausted a great deal of the time. For some women exercise can become an addiction (incredible as it may seem) and must be dealt with like any other addiction.

It's like the story of Goldilocks who found that the porridge was either 'too hot, too cold or just right.' Find the activity level that's 'just right' for you to increase your health, energy and vitality. It's important to keep an appropriate level of physical activity or exercise as part of your life because even moderate changes away from a sedentary lifestyle bring benefits. But you're thinking, I have no time for this, I never was an athlete! Do not fear. There are ways to put physical activity into your life that will be fun and something you will look forward to!

Exercise improves mood and intelligence! A study of 16,466 retired female nurses aged 70-81 found that even women who walked a leisurely 90 minutes a week did better on tests for mental function than less active women. Exercise also improves symptoms of menopause. According to Health Canada, physical inactivity makes your body age faster, something that women do not want!

A study at a university in Japan also concluded that exercise increases intelligence, our cognitive powers, helps to maintain our weight, builds bone, increases the 'feel good' endorphins to your brain, as well as reduces stress and anxiety. Frazzled Woman, physical activity reduces the stress chemicals that rage through your body such as cortisol or adrenaline. Exercise decreases depression! Yes! Exercise increases oxygen to the brain. You'll feel happier and in a better mood. So get moving today.

Even the busiest people can make room in their schedule for physical activity. Those who say they have no time for exercise are usually the most stressed. Pretend it's recess! Check out your daily or weekly schedule and look for or make opportunities to be more active, even fifteen minute spurts of energy. Every little bit helps! Instead of using your car or public transportation, you can walk, cycle, jog, or skate to work, to the store for errands, or to your place of worship. Too often we drive to the corner store without thinking about it. Tires have replaced our legs!

Consider the following suggestions for better health and wellness:

- Park the car or get off the bus farther away from your destination.
- Take the stairs instead of an elevator or escalator.
- Play with children or pets. Kids know how to be physically active, and walking the dog is great exercise.
- Try physical activity before work. If early morning finds you too tired, take a brisk walk inside your home or around the block after you get home.
- Exercise while watching TV using hand weights, a stationary bicycle, a treadmill or stair climber. (Treadmills are too often used for clothes hangers.) Follow a TV or DVD exercise or yoga program.

- Put on some fast-paced music you enjoy and dance right in the privacy of your home! No one's watching, or if they are, they can join you. Join an aqua fit program for women if you like the water. Or do lengths at a community pool. Rake leaves. Clean the house (oh no, not that!). Vacuuming really works up a sweat and burns calories!
- Join a gym or if you live in a condo, use the equipment in your building. Buy exercise equipment to be used at home. The large exercise balls are an inexpensive way to exercise and come with instructions to help you get started.
- Start or join a walking club with neighbors, friends or co-workers.

Try something. It will get you out of the doldrums! You'll also tone up, lose weight and reduce stress! Make a commitment to yourself to do some form of exercise daily if only for fifteen minutes. Your stamina and energy levels will increase. You'll look better and feel better.

Three Components of Fitness:

a) **Strength training** — activities against resistance to strengthen muscles and bones and to improve posture. Lifting weights or even raising soup cans above your head helps to build muscle and prevent or reverse osteoporosis. As you slowly build your strength, muscle endurance will follow.

b) **Aerobic Capacity/Endurance** — continuous activities for your heart, lungs and circulatory system that get your heart rate up. You can walk, use a treadmill, climb stairs, and dance. When you consistently do these types of activities you'll be more able to chase the dog or run after your kids without getting out of breath. Even short spurts are effective and you can increase your level as you go, building your lung capacity. Fifteen minutes of stair climbing a day equals 35-40 minutes a day of walking.

c) **Flexibility** — gentle reaching, bending and stretching activities that keep your muscles relaxed and joints mobile. Mobile joints help to keep a person independent in later life. The stretches after your workout attend to this important aspect of exercise.

Note: If you have injuries, check with your doctor, physiotherapist or chiropractor for directions on exercising. To improve posture, strength and mobility, I also recommend the Mitzvah Technique, the Alexander Technique or the Trager Approach.

Tips for getting started—and sticking with it:

- Find the types of exercise you like.
- Make a four-month commitment.
- Develop a weekly plan: set goals.
- Practice moderation, gradualism and patience.
- If it's helpful, exercise with a friend or group.
- Introduce variety: walk one day, swim the next.
- If you miss a session or two, do not quit altogether.
- Be aware of negative self-talk about exercise.
- START!

Try some form of physical activity! If you don't know where to start, and if budget allows, hire a personal trainer for a few sessions to get on the right track. You will look better and feel better, reduce stress and add life to your years.

If you're flexible, limber, and well warmed up each day, your body can readily move through its range of motion with a minimum effort on your part. But if inflexible, cold muscles are asked to work to or beyond their maximum to accomplish what should be an ordinary task, your risk of injury will be increased.

Benefits of stretching: Three cheers for flexibility!

- Stretching is an important part of an overall fitness program of exercise and optimum diet for strengthening and conditioning your body.
- A decline in flexibility, often evidenced by stiff muscles, means a decline in stability and balance, making a fall more likely. Correct stretching can increase flexibility, improve cardiovascular function, reduce back pain, help ease osteoarthritis, prevent tendonitis and protect against carpal tunnel syndrome.
- A good stretching program brings easy movement and protection from injury even to those who rarely exercise. Bouncing stretches have been cited as dangerous, yet some yoga classes instruct participants to gently bounce when stretching. There are two schools of thought for timing stretches. Phil and Jim Wharton, the authors of *The Wharton's Stretch Book* recommend two-second stretches repeated five to ten times. The American Council of Sports Medicine recommends at least ten seconds per stretch for improved flexibility. Find what's best for you.
- Stretching may be uncomfortable, especially if you are working on a particularly stiff joint but it should never be painful. Listen to your body and judge what sensations are signals that something is wrong. Make sure your positioning of stretches is correct.

Easy exercises on an airplane or sitting at your desk!*
This form of multi-tasking is okay:

Leg, foot stretch

Place a cushion at your lower back. Flex each foot so heels are touching the floor and toes are raised as high as possible. Then shift so toes are on the floor and the heels are raised. Quickly shift from heel to toe, for eight counts. Breathe deeply.

Isometrics for arms, upper chest

Press down hard on armrests; hold for count of five. Grab under the armrest and pull up, hold for count of five. Repeat five times.

Lower back stretches

Clasp both hands around one knee; pull knee up to your chest. Hold for a count of five. Repeat with the other leg. You can teach the person beside you the stretches too if they think you've lost it!

Exercises for the shoulders and arms

Link fingers, hands in front of chest. Lift hands and arms up above head. Reach for the roof. Breathe in deeply. Hold for three seconds. Bring hands down behind head and hold for three seconds. Repeat whole sequence three times.

Neck stretches

a) **forward and back:** Tuck your chin and gently bend your head forward, chin to chest. Gently bend your head backward to its limit. Repeat five times.

b) **ear to shoulder:** Stretch your neck to the side to the right as far as possible, to try to touch ear to shoulder. (Do not overstretch.) Stretch neck to the left as far as possible to touch ear to shoulder. Repeat five times.

c) **side to side:** Turn head to the right as far as possible to bring chin over shoulder and hold for three to five seconds. Do not raise your shoulder. Repeat on the left side. Do five times.

* Excerpts from "How to Exercise on an Airplane", *USA Today*, W. Bryant May 19, 1998

Inactivity is as harmful to your health as smoking.

According to Health Canada, physical inactivity makes your body age faster (the best reason of all to exercise!). Additionally, the World Health Organization states that sitting or lying for long periods is a serious health risk. Good reason to get off the couch!

What will motivate you? Well, you've heard the reasons why we should add physical activity to our lives, so now, let's get moving. Making time in your calendar or changing sedentary habits is the first step. Frazzled Women are obviously capable of so much that embarking on this important health buffer should be a cinch. Physical activity is an investment in your health. You will get a large pay-off.

No pill holds as much promise for sustained health as a lifetime program of regular physical activity. Sigh...

PART TWO of the Health Trio: Wondrous Sleep

Sleep refreshes us like nothing else. It can be occasionally elusive, almost always comforting, and definitely essential to our survival. And although we spend 33% of our lives asleep, we barely give it a moment's notice...until we **can't** sleep. Then we think about it to the point of obsession. Those nights lying awake, tossing, turning are torture for the Frazzled Woman who knows she needs sleep.

Adequate sleep protects against distress and is vital for rejuvenating the mind and body, something the Frazzled Woman definitely wants! Sleep deficiency causes irritability and stress damage, anxiety, depression, early aging, fatigue, disturbed thinking and physical disorders, aches and pains. Most adults function best when getting about eight hours of sleep, but individual differences occur. However, most of us feel terrible when we don't get enough sleep.

Sleep problems have become epidemic, affecting 1/3 of the population. If you're over 50, lack of quality sleep can have very serious consequences beyond daytime fatigue, either causing major health issues or making existing conditions worse. A study published in the *Archives of Internal Medicine* by researchers at Brigham and Women's Hospital in Boston found that too little sleep may raise your risk of developing heart disease.

Several reports from the Harvard-run Nurses' Health Study have linked insufficient or irregular sleep to increased risk for colon cancer, breast cancer, heart disease and diabetes. Other research groups have subsequently found clues that might explain why sleep disruption affects crucial hormones and proteins that play roles in these diseases.

Get some shut-eye! One can't function (or live) without it.

Physiologic studies suggest that a sleep deficit may put the body into a state of high alert, thereby increasing the production of stress hormones and driving up blood pressure, a major risk factor for heart attacks and strokes. Moreover, people who are sleep-deprived have elevated levels of substances in the blood that indicate a heightened state of inflammation in the body, which has also recently emerged as a major risk factor for heart disease, stroke, cancer and diabetes.

"Lack of sleep disrupts every physiologic function in the body. We have nothing in our biology that allows us to adapt to this behavior (losing sleep)," says Eve Van Cauter of the University of Chicago. The amount of necessary sleep varies from person to person, with some folks able to breeze through their days on just a few hours' slumber and others barely functioning without a full 10 hours. Experts tell us that most people apparently need between about seven to nine hours, with studies indicating that an increased risk for disease starts to kick in when people get less than six or seven.

Chronic diseases and medical conditions can and often do lead to sleep disorders–heartburn, reflux, heart problems, arthritis, osteoporosis, and cancer. Other conditions that also lead to sleep problems include back pain, headaches, muscle aches, leg cramps, sinus pain and restless leg syndrome.

Certainly, frazzled lifestyles lead to sleep problems. We are not giving our minds or bodies time to relax.

Do you have sleep apnea? Sleep apnea is a condition that causes airways to become blocked during sleep, triggering breathing to stop periodically. People with sleep apneas don't even realize their sleep is being disrupted. When depression or anxiety appears to be the reason for the disorder, psychotherapy will be advised as treatment. Sleep medications may also be prescribed on a short term basis to complement the therapy. Some dentists specialize in particular mouth bite plates fitted on the teeth that can alter the flow of air to offer relief for sleep apnea.

If you suffer from sleep loss on a regular basis, you may need to make an appointment with a sleep clinic. They can analyze your heart rate, breathing patterns and oxygen levels to find out if you're holding your breath (sleep apnea) or not getting enough deep sleep.

Signs of a sleeping disorder:
Difficulty concentrating
Excessive daytime sleepiness
Lack of energy and motivation
Loss of memory
Loud snoring
Morning headaches
Reduced sense of well-being
Trouble falling and staying asleep

What keeps you from sleeping?
- If you have heartburn that keeps you up, learn the source and treat it.
- Precipitating factors can include interpersonal or financial stress, loss of a job.
- Factors associated with chronic insomnia can include medical or psychiatric conditions, sleep/wake cycle disturbances, medications, substance abuse, or primary sleep disorders.
- Sleep problems could be an early manifestation of depression and can possibly cause other psychiatric conditions as well.
- Pre-menopause or post-menopause can precipitate insomnia.

For good health we must go through the sleep cycles. Before falling into actual sleep as we know it, the body starts slowing down in preparation. All people fall asleep with tense muscles, their eyes moving erratically. Usually as a person becomes sleepier, the body starts slowing down. Eye movements slow to a roll.

Since the early 20th century, the state we refer to as human sleep is actually a succession of five recurring stages throughout the night: four non-REM stages and the REM stage.

REM sleep (rapid eye movement) sleep is marked by extensive physiological changes, such as quick breathing, increased brain activity, eye movement (when eyes are closed), and muscle relaxation.

The quality of sleep changes with transitions from one sleep stage into another. Every stage of sleep is important even though they do not progress in a predictable pattern sequence of 1 − 5. Often other stages are called in within the cycles so that the body can have restorative, healing sleep. The body is truly remarkable.

Stage 1 is the beginning of the sleep cycle, and is a relatively light stage of sleep. In this brief period of 5-10 minutes, the brain produces very slow brain waves—high amplitude theta waves.

Stage 2 is the second stage of sleep and lasts for approximately 20 minutes. The brain begins to produce bursts of rapid, rhythmic brain wave activity. Body temperature starts to decrease and heart rate begins to slow.

Stage 3 produces deep, slow brain waves known as delta waves, a transitional period between light sleep and a very deep sleep.

Stage 4 finds people in a deep sleep, producing slow delta waves. This stage lasts for approximately 30 minutes.

Stage 5 is known for its REM sleep, rapid eye movement. Dreaming occurs during this stage. Along with eye movement, respiration rate and brain activity increase.

One can clearly see that if a person does not sleep well, the intricate workings of these five stages and their cycles are likely interrupted. A Frazzled Woman working into the night can likely go one night without sleeping well, or think she can. However, by the second night without adequate sleep—it's damage control! Watch out for her behind the wheel!

Which mechanisms in the body control sleep? Adrenalin levels are higher during the day to keep you stimulated. As you start to wind down, adrenalin levels fall and serotonin levels rise. Melatonin, another neurotransmitter kicks in. Both melatonin and serotonin are made from the amino acid tryptophan. Melatonin, produced in the pineal gland in the center of the brain, regulates the sleep/wake cycle.

Many women become serotonin deficient. Without enough serotonin you don't make enough melatonin. Without melatonin, it's difficult to get to sleep and stay asleep.

Some foods make you sleepy. Adequate amounts of Vitamin B6 and tryptophan are needed to send you off for a good night's sleep. Foods high in tryptophan are chicken, turkey, cheese, tuna, tofu, eggs, nuts, seeds, milk, lettuce and oats.

Supplementing 5-HTP or melatonin itself is effective. 5-HTP (hydroxytryptophan) is the direct precursor of serotonin and by supplementing it you can increase levels of melatonin and serotonin. 100-200 mg of 5-HTP a half hour before sleep can help you to get a good night's rest. Tryptophan, at 2,000 mg a night (prescription necessary), also works well.

Check with your doctor or health care professional before

trying 5-HTP or melatonin. Melatonin is a neurotransmitter and not a nutrient; it's helpful, but must be used cautiously. Too much can cause diarrhea, constipation, nausea, dizziness, reduced libido, headaches, depression and nightmares. Under the care of a health professional, trying 5-HTP or melatonin for a month can bring you back into balance, to re-establish proper sleep patterns.

A calcium/magnesium combined supplement, (600 mg. of calcium and 400 mg of magnesium) at bedtime helps people unwind. Valerian (either in tea or in capsule form) is often called 'Nature's Valium.' It can interact with alcohol and other sedative drugs and should NOT be taken in combination with them.

Other natural sleep aids include passion flower and St. John's Wort (Hypericum), which has both serotonin and melatonin enhancing effects. Passion flower is helpful for anxiety, stress and insomnia. It calms the nerves when a person is nervous and excited and can't sleep. Passion flower is not recommended for usage during pregnancy and lactation. Hops, in use for centuries as a mild sedative and sleeping aid, work on the central nervous system.

Combinations of these herbs, together with 5-HTP, are the most effective natural sleep promoters of all.

Note: Check with your health care provider to find out what is best for you. **It is unwise to self-medicate.** Over the counter aids, even natural ones, must not be taken casually.

Natural ways to fall asleep:

1. It's a good idea to spend the hour before going to bed unwinding and mentally separating yourself from the day. Cue yourself that it's time to get sleepy with rituals such as brushing your teeth, locking doors, closing curtains. If possible, go to bed at the same time each night.

2. Limit your caffeine, nicotine and alcohol consumption, especially after 6:00 p.m. Alcohol may help you get to sleep but often will awaken you in the middle of the night.
3. Exercise each day (not within two hours of bedtime) to release pent-up stress.
4. Try to get at least 15 minutes of sunlight each day to properly set bio-rhythms.
5. Listen to a relaxation tape or soothing, mellow music.
6. Do deep, slow, rhythmic breathing. Breathe slowly, as if you were already asleep.
7. If you have the day's activities marching through your mind, imagine writing each one on a blackboard, and then erasing the lines you've written with a brush or soft cloth.
8. Ensure that you sleep in a dark room to boost melatonin production in the brain.
9. Don't eat dinner too late in the evening. However, a small snack a half hour before bed to prevent low blood sugar may help ease you into sleep.
10. Warm (not hot) baths are relaxing and may induce sleep.
11. Stop worrying about getting to sleep and eventually you will.
12. Get up if you cannot sleep; read or relax until you feel sleepy.
13. Count your blessings.

PART THREE of the Health Trio: Eat Well!

You are what you eat! So what do your eating habits say about you?

In our modern era of fast food, microwave food and junk food, the fact that we must have nutrients to power our mind and body seems to be ignored. The primary method of getting nutrients is through our food sources—what you decide to feed your body. And while we all have compulsions about certain foods, you do have a choice of what goes into your mouth. You can still eat well even if you're busy! Food is more than nourishment. It's a representation of our culture; it's what brings people together for social gatherings. It's love.

Take-Away Gems

- Design a physical activity program that makes sense for you and your schedule.
- Make fitness or just moving your body part of everyday living.
- Include stretches in your daily routine or while sitting at your desk.
- Find an activity you enjoy and you're more apt to stick to it.
- Become aware of how many hours per night you are sleeping.
- Wind down an hour or so before bed; drink calming teas.
- Don't work during the night.
- Get help if you have sleep apnea or a sleep disorder.
- Have a nap later in the day if you are exhausted.

Everyone loved you frazzled, but the real you is ready to make her debut. You'll leave them breathless!

CHAPTER SEVEN

This Is Your Brain Speaking
Feed Me, I'm Hungry!

Yesterday, she fed me pizza and fries. The redeeming factor was the ketchup, even though it's high in sugar and makes me crazy for about a half hour. However, it does contain tomatoes, which are high in lycopene, a wonderful antioxidant. So I guess I shouldn't complain. But my circuits are malfunctioning; I'm rambling. I can't remember squat. Today if The Frazzled Woman isn't running too fast, I might get a real dinner with some grilled chicken, brown rice and broccoli! Who am I kidding? If

I'm lucky, I'll probably get a greasy hamburger and a diet soda. (Sigh) I can't go on. I'm walking out. Oh, I can't. I'm her brain.

Food and Mood are Connected

Can food choices be the culprit for bad moods, low energy and fuzzy thinking? Do you sometimes feel you have 'brain fog' after you eat? Do you get up in the morning feeling tired even though you've slept all night? Do you find yourself getting anxious a few hours after you've skipped lunch or after a high sugar content meal? If so, you're not alone.

The Frazzled Woman has little time to think about food for herself. If she has children and a partner/spouse, she organizes breakfast and lunch for the kids and plans what she will put on the dinner table for the family. But for herself, she mostly grabs meals and snacks without much thought. Or if she does manage healthy meals, she often eats or gulps on the run. There's no pause for digestion.

Coffee is the main pick-me-up in the morning and again in late afternoon. Cravings? They're so strong, they send The Frazzled Woman straight to the cookie jar or a drive-in donut depot! If this is you, it's quite possible you need a health tune-up.

This chapter reveals the impact that food choices have on the brain and how psychological and physical dependence develops. Best of all, it lists foods to boost moods, energy and concentration to keep stress at an arm's length.

A Bitter/Sweet Tale

Back in 1986, I was stranded in a snowstorm while on a business trip, in a little town far from home. Miserable and cold,

I trudged though the snow to a corner store and bought a huge chocolate bar. The store didn't have my favourite dark chocolate, so I had to settle for milk chocolate. I said to myself, "I'll have a couple of bites and save the rest for later." Ha! The first few squares were sweet, delicious and comforting—you know what I mean. Of course, I ate the whole thing. An hour or so later, I felt guilty, depressed and nauseous. I could feel my heart pounding, likely from the sugar rush or excess caffeine in such a large bar of chocolate.

So why didn't the chocolate bar make me feel better? I wondered if there could be a connection to the food I ate and my increasingly plunging mood that evening.

"Let food be thy medicine and medicine be thy food."
— Hippocrates

Hippocrates is known as the Father of Medicine. I doubt if his wisdom would apply to our present day fast food culture: the cola drinks, burgers, fries, coffee and donuts.

Just as food can be nourishment as well as healing medicine, so too can it be a profound detriment to our health, both physically and mentally. Food has powerful effects on the mind, which people often forget is part of the body; they both need nourishment.

Nutrients, such as vitamins and minerals, are able to cross the blood-brain barrier that protects our brains from bacteria and other invaders.

Why the Brain is Dependent on Nutrition

The brain's neurotransmitters are fueled by nutrients, which must be constantly replenished. A correct balance of mineral electrolytes is needed to enable the axons to correctly transfer neural messages. The brain also requires 20% of the body's supply of oxygen and glucose, along with nutrients, in order to convert that glucose into energy. In other words, for every meal you eat, a good portion of your intake gets converted into brain energy!

Our systems have a demand for a steady supply of proteins, vitamins, minerals, unrefined carbohydrates, essential fatty acids and enzymes for adequately functioning circulatory, immune, digestive, respiratory and endocrine systems. **And the brain is the master control.**

Oddly enough, we are living in an era when nutrition is often referred to as alternative therapy. Very few nutrition courses are taught in medical schools. Patients are given special diets by their doctors only if they develop an illness such as high cholesterol, diabetes or if they suffer from obesity. Food plans for the rest of the population, emphasizing whole food nutrition, are rarely discussed.

However, many doctors, scientists, biochemists and some psychiatrists say that the link between food and mood is undeniable. A report by the Mental Health Foundation in the U.K., called *Feeding Minds, Impact of Fresh, Healthy Foods on Learning and Behavior* is available online. Especially for teens, the YouTube video *Impact of Fresh, Healthy Foods on Learning and Behavior* is another great resource. A documentary film, *Food Matters*, is a hard-hitting fast-paced look at our current state of health. It explores the safe, cheap and effective use of nutrition and supplementation for preventing and often reversing the underlying causative aspects of illness. Additional information about food, nutrients and their effects on mental health can be found at orthomed.org.

A turkey sandwich, a donut or an apple? All the food you eat becomes energy for your body so that you can stay alive. Are you running on high or low octane fuel in your tank? Or are you chugging along on fumes? "We are what we eat" means that we function well or poorly because of the nutrients we consume.

Nutrients power the mitochondria,
the energy factory of every cell of the body.

Why don't we eat what's good for us? For most people, food is more than nourishment. Opening the fridge after dinner generally is a hunt for comfort food, often something sweet. Some folks reach for salty snacks such as potato chips. We eat certain foods because they evoke happy memories. My father worked long hours and on Sundays he took me for a walk. That was our time together for the week. Our destination was the candy store, where I could choose an ice cream cone or chocolate bar. That association of sweets and love stayed with me for a long time. My allowance as a child was spent on candy. A subsequent chocolate and sweets addiction lasted for much of my adult life until I faced serious health-related issues.

We eat to be social. What's a celebration without food? We also eat foods that are familiar to us because of what our parents or other members of our culture ate. Cooking, family recipes and your choice of foods are strongholds of self-expression. When I ask clients to try different foods, often it's as though I'm asking them to fly to the moon! Many people eat the same foods each and every day of their lives and have a difficult time altering their habits. But I can assure you that from my own personal experience over time, it's possible to improve eating habits.

What you put into your mouth has a profound effect on how you think and feel. Both intellectually and culturally we tend to ignore the role of nutrition in mental health.

In my work as a holistic nutritionist providing individual nutritional consulting for patients of four medical doctors, I find patients' health improves with the addition of a wholesome diet suited to their particular needs. Whether patients have migraine headaches, a mental disorder or blood sugar problems, everyone can enjoy increased energy and reduction of their symptoms through improved dietary plans. Attention to possible food allergies is important. One of the doctors for whose patients I prepare food plans is a psychiatrist. She emphasizes nutrition for her patients, and she finds that with it, their medications work more effectively. An individualized allergen-free diet with the addition of certain supplements such as the B vitamins, vitamin C, minerals such as zinc, calcium and magnesium, amino acids or hormones can greatly improve mental health. This evidence based treatment is called orthomolecular medicine.

Orthomolecular Treatments of Mental Illness

The word orthomolecular was coined by Nobel Laureate Linus Pauling. 'Ortho' means to straighten and 'molecular' refers to using correct molecules for each person. Orthomolecular treatments provide the brain and the body with the best possible biochemical environment, especially with those substances normally found in the body such as vitamins, minerals, amino acids, essential fatty acids and other nutrients. They are administered according to the individual needs of the patient and are safe to use with medications. A holistic diet avoiding allergens is considered to be an important part of the therapy. Treatment for additional disorders such as low blood sugar, allergies, and thyroid problems are included when necessary.

The brain is highly dependent on thyroid hormone for the regulation of dopamine, norepinephrine, and serotonin pathways. Many outstanding studies report the efficacy of thyroid therapy using desiccated thyroid or thyroxine with B-complex, which can lead to a remarkable recovery of some serious forms of mental illness.[4]

Let's look at 'simple' hypoglycemia. Abnormally low blood sugar (an inadequate supply of glucose to the brain) can cause an individual to become depressed, apathetic, get the shakes, become irritable, even black out. If that same person also suffers anxiety, bipolar disorder, depression or schizophrenia, the untreated hypoglycemia can sharply exacerbate symptoms of the mental illness. Eating every few hours and making sure there are small (but adequate) amounts of protein at each meal along with other essential fats and complex carbohydrates can calm the hypoglycemic effects and restore one's balance.

On the other hand, if blood sugar is too elevated (hyperglycemia), then an individual who additionally has a mental illness can experience a racing heart or become hyper, manic and irrational. Further, if he/she is also drinking a pot of coffee a day or one of those large bottles of cola, the caffeine (and sugar) will also wildly escalate mood extremes. These disturbed blood sugar regulations (dysglycemia) are usually associated with a lifetime of poor dietary habits and choices, highlighted by the over-consumption of refined carbohydrates and poor quality fats. Type 2 diabetes reduced insulin sensitivity can be the undesirable outcome. Therapeutic replacement of insulin often becomes necessary.

For those people who are taking medication for mood disorders or psychosis, it is important to limit the numbers of servings of starchy foods such as bread, potatoes, white rice,

---

4   Danziger, L: Thyroid therapy of schizophrenia. Dis Nerv. Syst. 1958; 19(9); 373-378.

pasta, soft drinks (pop and soda) and sweets. For many people taking these medications, too many high calorie, starchy choices can escalate weight and lead to blood sugar problems.

Orthomolecular treatments have been used successfully and safely since the '50's, when extensive research was conducted by Abram Hoffer, MD, PhD and his research team of thirty. Their work took place in four psychiatric hospitals and three other psychiatric wards in Saskatchewan, Canada. Eight double blind research studies showed positive results for using forms of niacin and other nutrients in the treatment of schizophrenia. Thousands of other research studies using a variety of vitamins, minerals, fish oils, and amino acids have been done since that time with even better results for those with schizophrenia and other forms of mental illnesses. People suffering with depression, schizo-affective disorder, bipolar disorder, anxiety, dementia and autism can be helped with this safe adjunct treatment.

"The four elements of optimum treatment for those with schizophrenia include: shelter, good food, respectful care, orthomolecular medicine."[5] While orthomolecular treatments are not widespread, interest is steadily growing. Their applications are now used in 37 countries. Orthomolecular doctors, other health professionals and patients report better outcomes with the addition of orthomolecular treatments. Check orthomed.org for the Journal of Orthomolecular Medicine and the International Schizophrenia Foundation (ISF), organizations which promote orthomolecular treatments worldwide in order for people with mental illnesses to lead healthy and independent lives. The ISF's publication list includes many books and research papers about the effectiveness of various nutrients and their safety for those with all mental health issues. Research papers at no cost are available on the ISF website. To view the

5   A. Hoffer, MD, PhD, *Mental Health Regained, 18 Personal Stories of Recovery,* International Schizophrenia Foundation, 2007, p.9

15 minute clip of the film documentary *Masks of Madness: Science of Healing* narrated by and featuring Margot Kidder along with recovered patients and orthomolecular doctors, go to www.orthomed.org/isf/isfmasks.html. More research about the effectiveness of nutritional treatments for mental illnesses is available in traditional journals on Medline.

If you are taking medication for mental health issues, your doctor can only be pleased that you are assuming some personal responsibility to improve your health through dietary means. Change isn't easy, but with the support of family, friends and an empathetic health care team, you can break through cravings and old habits to experience an improved state of well-being. Diet and orthomolecular treatments can be used safely and effectively with medication under the care of a qualified health care professional. Contact the International Schizophrenia Foundation (ISF) for a list of orthomolecular physicians/health care professionals located in your area or visit helpyourselfcommunity.org for podcasts and events for the public. You can email centre@orthomed.org and ask about orthomolecular testing and treatment centers in the U.S. and Canada. Many orthomolecular doctors work in conjunction with a person's present psychiatrist. The ISF conducts doctor training programs for orthomolecular treatments and holds annual conferences in Canada.

A healthful diet is an important part of orthomolecular treatment since optimizing one's nutrients to meet individual requirements is necessary for the proper functioning of the body and mind. To their detriment, many people neglect the quality or proper quantity of their food intake.

Does this sound like you? "I hardly eat anything!" Without enough calories (from the right sources of food), you'll be tired all the time. Do you skip breakfast or lunch or both? If so, by 3:00 p.m. your blood sugar will be low. You may start to shake. Your brain has been deprived of nutrients; thus, your attention span becomes limited. You forget things. You can hardly wait to get your hands on a muffin and coffee. Missing meals encourages carbohydrate cravings. You may have a hard time curbing your all-evening snack attacks.

Human beings need energy to breathe, move, pump blood and think. Survival depends on it. The number of calories in any food is a measure of its potential energy release during digestion. A gram of carbohydrates has 4 calories, a gram of protein has 4 calories and a gram of fat has 9 calories. All foods are compiled of one or more of these three essential building blocks. If you know the measure of carbohydrates, fats and proteins in any given food, you know how many calories, or how much energy, you are accessing. Sedentary workers obviously need fewer calories than physical laborers, but they both need the right intake of performance energy.

The number of calories you should eat each day also depends on your age, sex, and body size. According to the U.S. Department of Health and Human Services, a woman between the ages of 31 and 50 who is of normal weight and moderately active should eat about 2,000 calories each day. Fit, exercising women may need more calories than the average recommendation, and extremely overweight women require fewer. It's therefore easy to see why fewer calories, combined with exercise, reduce body fat. Not only do these health strategies assist weight control, they also reduce stress.

Food is fuel, a source of vitality. Many people who eat (and live) on the run often disregard their need for sustained, high energy fuel. If you're eating mostly empty calories–sugar, sodium, and other chemically engineered foods—at the end of the digestion period your body has wasted the energy it took for the process. It gets back very little nutrition for all its trouble and you're exhausted.

Our bodies utilize calories through metabolic processes. Enzymes break down the carbohydrates into glucose and other sugars. The fats get broken into glycerol and fatty acids; proteins break down into amino acids. These molecules are then transported through the bloodstream to your cells for immediate use or are sent on to the final stage of metabolism in which they react with oxygen to release their stored energy.

Even though we live in a weight-obsessed culture, we generally consume too many calories due to high intake of fast foods, sugar and large portions. If you are one of life's Frazzled Women who would rather thrive than merely survive know that smart dietary* choices will start you on your way.

*A note about the word 'diet': Do not confuse this word with a tedious weight loss regime! The word strikes misery in the hearts of many because it has become commonly associated with weight loss. Diet simply means your choices of food and drink, for whatever reason: weight loss, growth, building stamina or just everyday meals; it can be good, mediocre, or downright inadequate. The healthy diet recommended in this book is about balanced meals and snacks chosen for vitality and energy. Following an appropriate diet will stabilize your weight naturally with well-portioned, whole food choices. Include adequate exercise and you'll have a win-win combination.

Nutrients—The Foundation of a Good Diet

'Good Mood' Protein

Protein gives the body the building blocks it needs to repair and rebuild, and it also serves as a source of energy. It is made up of fragments known as amino acids. Some amino acids can have a direct effect on levels of certain brain chemicals such as serotonin. Eating foods naturally high in tryptophan (fish, chicken, meat, eggs, dairy food, legumes, beans, tofu) can improve mood as the tryptophan is converted by the body to serotonin (the 'happy' neurotransmitter). Serotonin elevates mood, self-esteem, feelings of optimism and induces calm feelings and sleep. Foods such as bananas, walnuts and avocado also provide some ready-made serotonin.

Tryptophan and its co-worker, serotonin, create good moods.

Other neurotransmitters such as dopamine get boosted by foods such as chicken, turkey, cottage cheese, duck, eggs, walnuts and yogurt. Vegetarians need to attend to their protein needs. Vegetarian proteins can be found in tofu, tempeh, additional soy products, beans, lentils, spirulina and other seaweeds. Sometimes B12 supplements are recommended for those vegan vegetarians eating no animal proteins (such as cheese, eggs or fish) in order to ensure good brain health and prevent muscle wasting. People who may not be adequately digesting their proteins can benefit from B12 supplementation. Testing for B12 deficiency is available; check with your doctor or health care professional. A lack of adequate B12 can be a forerunner to mental illness.

Basic protein sources: meat, fish, eggs, cheese, peas, beans and nuts. Most proteins also contain fat such as the fat already in meat, fish and eggs. Many nuts are high in protein, but beware: nuts also contain high levels of fat and calories. The protein in nuts is less adequate than the protein in meats, fish or eggs. For example, after eating the small amount of protein provided in a peanut butter sandwich at lunch, an hour or so later you may find yourself losing brain power.

Nut protein is more complete when combined with other plant foods at the same meal. For the purposes of balancing meals and snacks, consider nuts as a 'combination food' of protein and fat—mostly healthy fat, **to be eaten in moderation.**

'Good Mood' Carbohydrates

Carbohydrates can either be simple or complex. There is sugar in all carbohydrates: it's all about amounts that our bodies can handle since some sugars found in carbohydrates are better for us than others.

a) Simple Carbohydrates

Simple carbohydrates are made up of one or two sugar molecules linked together and are used to fuel our bodies. Examples of simple carbohydrates include glucose, fructose (fruit sugar), sucrose (table sugar) and galactose (the sugar found in milk). Simple sugars are used as ingredients in candy, ice cream, cookies and other sweets. **Many people are eating too much of this type of sugar.**

Simple sugars also occur naturally in fruits and lesser amounts are found in vegetables. Pure plant foods, vegetables and some fruits in their whole form are better carbohydrates for the body than a steady stream of simple carbohydrates found in processed goodies or an overabundance of fruit. (Yes, a person can eat too much fruit.)

Refined sugar is a **simple carbohydrate**, the type responsible for creating cravings and dependency; it is found primarily in most processed or refined foods—'junk foods.' These carbohydrates have short-chained sugar molecules and are digested very quickly. Examples of both refined and 'natural' simple carbohydrates include table sugar, fruit juice, milk, yogurt, honey, molasses, maple syrup and brown sugar. Some people are more sensitive to sugar than others. Repeatedly eating too much sugar eventually keeps blood sugar levels too high, which deteriorates organs and causes inflammation to the body.

When you eat (or drink) a **simple carbohydrate** or a **simple sugar**—whether it is a can of soda, a scoop of fat-free ice cream, or even a glass of orange juice—all of the ingested sugar quickly **rushes into your bloodstream**. You likely will feel a quick rush of energy to your brain and body. Your body then promptly calls on the pancreas to produce additional insulin to remove the excess sugar from your blood. And for the moment, the insulin does its job and the results are a significantly lower blood sugar. But then you may get a sense or feeling of needing more energy and calories. The feeling initiates a craving of more of the quick-release, simple sugars. The sugar craving cycle has begun.

Another hormone, glucagon comes into the digestive process to allow stored body fat to be released into the bloodstream (and eventually out of your body). Too much sugar not only produces insulin, but also essentially shuts off glucagon production—the fat release hormone. So your weight increases from eating too much sugar. If you must have simple sugar (a cookie or other dessert), add a protein (such as a piece of cheese or nuts) which will help to slow down the sugar's release into the bloodstream, and reduce the insulin/glucagon effect.

While fruits are often referred to as simple natural sugars, they at least give the body nutrients–vitamins and minerals necessary for good health. Your **glycemic index (GI)** , is a measure of the effects of carbohydrates on your blood glucose (sugar) levels: you'll want to choose foods on a slow, or 'low' GI scale. Fruits that are low on the glycemic index and that have high nutrient value include blackberries, cherries, cranberries, (not dried and sweetened with sugar), grapefruit, kiwi, lemon, melon, peaches, pears, plums, raspberries and strawberries.

For most women, three servings (½ cup per serving) a day of fruit will give your body a natural boost and the necessary nutrients your body needs. Tiny women may only need two servings per day. Natural sugars in fruit have a gentler effect on blood sugar levels than refined sugar.

You can get too much of a good thing. Even natural foods such as corn syrup, fruit juices, and honey contain a form of sugar called **glucose** that is absorbed directly through the stomach wall and rapidly released into the bloodstream. It's possible though, to overdo it. Ingesting too much of these 'natural foods' can still be harmful by raising blood sugar levels too high. Products made from corn often increase carbohydrate cravings. Can you eat just one corn chip?

Glucose travels along your bloodstream, powering every cell, including those in your brain. Since your cellular neurons cannot store glucose, they depend on the bloodstream to deliver a steady supply of this necessary fuel for energy. Again, too much can compromise your brain's power to concentrate, remember, and learn.

b) Complex Carbohydrates

Complex carbohydrates are chains of three or more single sugar molecules linked together. Long chains of sugar molecules are called starches and they serve as the storage form of energy in plants and in turn give you energy. Frazzled Women 'on the go' need to have some complex carbs to sustain their busy lifestyles.

Unlike simple carbs, **complex carbs don't hit the bloodstream in a quick rush** as they take longer to digest. They are packed with fiber, vitamins and minerals. Examples include vegetables, whole grain breads, oatmeal, legumes, brown rice and whole wheat or other whole grain pasta. Green vegetables including broccoli, green beans and spinach contain less starch and more fiber. Other complex carbohydrates include asparagus, broccoli, cauliflower, onions, mushrooms, peppers and most varieties of dark green leafy vegetables. (On a daily basis, a woman should aim for at least double the servings of vegetables over fruit.)

'Veggie power' is very real and can transform your body.

Cellulose is another complex carbohydrate and helps give plants their shape. While most starches are fairly easy to digest, your body doesn't digest cellulose. It passes through the small intestine into the colon and the fiber it contains helps to keep the colon healthy. Some disorders like diverticulitis, constipation and irregularity may be traced to a lack of dietary fiber.

Because **complex carbohydrates** are more natural and beneficial to your system, you'll need to understand which choices to make. That's where complex carbohydrates excel because they are slow releasing, aiding the absorption of tryptophan (that 'good mood' chemical) into the brain.

Your mother was right when she told you to eat your oatmeal (whole grain, not instant). It has a low glycemic index; therefore, by its gradual release into your system, it not only kept you from being hungry all morning at school, but also kept your brain receptive to learning.

As an adult, you'll appreciate the fact that energy-dense, low GI foods produce only small fluctuations in blood glucose and insulin levels. They are recommended to combat against diabetes and heart disease by reducing cholesterol levels, and sustaining weight loss.

Some slow releasing 'carbs' with a low glycemic index (GI) include:

- Beans and legumes
- Oatmeal, other whole grains in moderation
- Green vegetables

For many, fruits with higher sugar content (and calories) such as banana, mango, apples, pears, raisins and dates need to be eaten in moderation. Other high starch carbohydrate plant foods such as white potatoes, sweet potatoes, brown rice, and winter squash should also be eaten in moderation to prevent weight gain and increased blood sugar levels. Again, the recommended amount depends upon your current weight and activity level. A half a banana, or a ½ cup or 2/3 cup of brown rice or small potato is generally enough for a meal's serving of complex carbs for most women eating three meals and one or two snacks in a day.

So, whether the Frazzled Woman eats a meal or snack of 100% complex carbohydrates, or even simple carbs such as candy, she still boosts the brain levels of the neurotransmitter serotonin. That's great because serotonin has a calming effect, **but if the source of relief is from high refined sugars**, that 'boost' lasts only for a short time, less than two hours—perhaps as brief as a half hour. Many people under emotional stress turn to quick sweets and starches such as donuts.

Now, what's wrong with a little ol' donut? Well, it works this way: Shortly after a sweet or starchy snack when serotonin levels decline, blood sugar drops and anxiety reappears. We need another big snack of sweets and can get caught up in the vicious cycle of anxiety and food induced sedation. Weight gain is the inevitable side effect of excess carbohydrate intake, along with the potential to raise triglyceride (a form of cholesterol) blood levels in some people. A continually high blood sugar (from too many carbs) can not only lead to diabetes, but also it can lead to high cholesterol.

Stick to natural, slow-releasing carbohydrates as they greatly help to stabilize blood sugar (and mood). GI food ratings can be found at: www.glycemicindex.com

Fats: The good, the bad and the shameful

The brain is composed of over 60% fat. Fatty acids (from fats) are what your brain needs to create cells to help you think and feel. Avoiding all fat can lead to anxiety and depression and other mental health problems. However, the brain needs to be nourished with the right kinds of fats. Eating the wrong ones—hydrogenated fats and too many fats from animals, for instance—is not good for the brain. However, some natural fat in organic eggs, grass-fed beef, organic chicken and small amounts of butter can be beneficial. Wild game such as duck and goose also contain healthy Omega 3 fats—even so, deep frying is not recommended.

Hydrogenated fats have been highly processed and get their name from the hydrogen that has been pumped into them. Hydrogenated fats are solid or semi-solid at room temperature and are found in margarine and in vegetable shortenings. These controversial fats and oils have been widely used in processed packaged foods such as cakes and cookies and other products of the food industry for the last 50 years, primarily to extend their shelf life. A loaf of bread made with hydrogenated oil can sit on the counter for weeks without fear of rancidity.

> *"Unfortunately, a longer life for*
> *the product may mean a shorter life for you."*
> — *Dean Ornish, MD and author*

After years of reports of the health hazards of trans fats, Food Boards in North America continued to allow them in a wide variety of processed food items. European countries banned these fats long before their North American counterparts finally conceded to begin similar programs.

Some major food chains in the U.S. and Canada have chosen to remove or reduce trans fats in their products. In some cases these changes have been voluntary. In other cases, however, food vendors have been targeted by legal action that has generated a lot of media attention and forced the issue.

It is great news that Health Canada is showing leadership by stepping up to the (dinner) plate under the direction of the Minister of Health and the Trans Fat Task Force to promote better heart health. Their recommended guidelines (initiated in June 2007) for companies and food manufacturers support the replacement of trans fats with healthier alternatives such as monounsaturated and polyunsaturated fats and restrict the replacement of trans fats with saturated fats. Health Canada aims to closely monitor the actions of the industry via the Trans Fat Monitoring Program to make sure that: 1) trans fat content of vegetable oils and soft, spreadable margarines do not exceed 2% of their total fat content; and 2) trans fat content for all foods be limited to 5% of the total fat content, including ingredients sold to restaurants. Grocery shoppers, and those eating fast food truly need to be vigilant until these recommendations are fully implemented (in all countries).

Trans fats are a health hazardous side effect of hydrogenation. Given that **HDL and LDL** (cholesterol) are both important markers for overall cardiovascular health, researchers have found that trans fatty acids significantly raise LDL cholesterol levels while lowering the HDL levels. In the Framingham Heart Study (a 40 year study covering 5,209 individuals living in Massachusetts) high LDL cholesterol levels combined with low HDL levels was indicative of coronary heart disease risk.

Not only are hydrogenated fats bad for your heart, but they are also bad for your brain.

Animal research carried out by scientists at the Medical University of South Carolina and a range of other studies have shown that these trans fats could contribute to learning and memory difficulties in the brain.

Cholesterol is a soft, waxy substance found among the lipids (fats) in the bloodstream and in all your body's cells. It's an important part of a healthy body because it's used to form cell membranes, some hormones, and other vital functions.

People acquire cholesterol in two ways. The body — mainly the liver — produces varying amounts. Foods also can contain cholesterol: a prime source is from animals (especially egg yolks, meat, poultry, shellfish and whole and reduced-fat milk and dairy products). Again, it's all about amounts. A little organic animal protein (2 – 3 oz. at a meal is okay. A fatty steak hanging over the plate each night may not be. Foods from plants (fruits, vegetables, grains, nuts and seeds) don't contain cholesterol. Balance is the key.

Keeping your LDL ("lousy" cholesterol) level on the low side can help prevent cholesterol from sticking to the artery walls thereby also lowering the risk for heart attack.

Keeping your higher HDL ("healthy" cholesterol) levels higher than your LDL is desirable and may decrease your risk of heart attack and stroke. HDLs contain more protein than fat and actually help to sweep away the "lousy" cholesterol in the bloodstream.

Triglycerides are a type of fat that is found in the blood. What you eat is converted to quick energy, but excess calories (including carbohydrates) are converted to triglycerides and are stored as fat. A normal amount is useful, but if you consistently consume more calories than you burn, you may have a high triglyceride count—putting your overall cholesterol count in danger and setting the stage for obesity and diabetes.

'Good Mood' Fats

Monounsaturated Fats support good moods. Myelin, the protective sheath that covers communicating neurons, is composed of 30% protein and 70% fat. One of the most common good mood fatty acids in myelin is oleic acid. Where can you find good fats such as oleic acid? Mono-unsaturated oleic acid is the main component of olive oil. You can also get it from the oils found in almonds, pecans, macadamias, peanuts, and avocados. (Avocados are delicious when used in a guacamole dip.)

Polyunsaturated Omega 3 fats are particularly important for heart and brain health. They are found in oil-rich fish such as salmon, mackerel and sardines along with pumpkin seeds, walnuts, ground flax seeds or their oils. Chia seeds, sea vegetables, and green leafy vegetables also contain this important fat as do readily available Omega 3 rich eggs. (The chickens that produce these eggs have been fed flax seed meal.)

"**Phospholipids** are the 'intelligent' fats in your brain. They are insulation experts, helping make up the myelin that sheathes all nerves and so promoting a smooth run for all the signals in the brain. Not only do phospholipids enhance your mood, mind and mental performance, they also protect against age-related memory decline and Alzheimer's disease. There are two kinds of phospholipids – phosphatidyl choline (PC) and phosphatidyl serine (PS). Supplementing phosphatidyl choline and phosphatidyl serine has some very positive benefits for your brain."[6]

"The richest sources of phospholipids in the average diet are egg yolks and organ meats. Nowadays we eat much less of both than we did a few decades ago. Since egg phobia set in, amid the unfounded fears that dietary cholesterol was the major cause of heart disease, our intake of phospholipids has gone down dramatically. Conversely, the number of people suffering from memory and concentration problems has gone up."[7]

6   P. Holford, *Optimum Nutrition for the Mind*, Judy Platkus Publishers 2003
7   P. Holford, p. 35

"Lecithin is the best source of phospholipids, and widely available in health food shops, sold either as lecithin granules or capsules."[8]

"The easiest and cheapest way to take this is to add a tablespoon of lecithin, or a heaped teaspoon of high-PC lecithin, to your cereal in the morning. Or you can take lecithin supplements."[9]

Polyunsaturated Omega 6 fats are healthy forms of fat found in nuts and seeds and other oils such as expeller cold-pressed sunflower or safflower oils.

Be aware that our modern supermarket diets, laden with the wrong oils, (especially those found in most packaged snack foods) contain **too much** Omega 6, often in highly processed forms, and not enough Omega 3 fats. Become a label reader. Look for cold-pressed oils (for freshness and to avoid rancidity), such as olive and walnut. Cold-pressed oils have not been heated to high temperatures and all the vitamins, minerals and benefits of the fresh oils are retained. We all know what happens to vegetables when they are cooked too long. They lose their bright colours and their nutrients.

These processed fats can become dangerous to our health. Many health experts feel these damaged fats are the reason for many of the rising health problems in our society.

No fat? Nancy is very proud because she seldom eats fat. However, she often feels down and moody. Sometimes she's edgy or hyper. If you are skimping on essential fatty acids— good, natural fats such as those contained in nuts, seeds, peanut butter, fish and their oils, olives, or olive oil—you too could develop mood swings, hyperactivity and depression as well as other physical ailments. Not enough of the right kind of fats creates stress.

8   P. Holford, p. 34
9   P. Holford, p. 35

What else does the brain need? Vitamins and minerals. The conversion of the tryptophan protein fragments into the good mood brain chemical serotonin is assisted by various 'co-factor' nutrients such as Vitamin C, Folic Acid, Vitamin B6, Biotin, Zinc and Selenium. These co-factor nutrients can be found in citrus fruits, avocados, leafy greens, fish, oats, sardines, and walnuts. The brain relies on micronutrients, the anti-oxidants from fruits and vegetables, to safeguard its cells from damage.

Inadequate intake of vitamins and minerals contributes to low energy, irritability, insomnia and anxiety. For example: B Vitamins help convert fat and protein to energy, including the production of adrenaline.

Under the advice of a health care professional, these vitamins and minerals can also be taken as supplements for those with deficiencies. Many people require a dosage of certain nutrients far beyond the Recommended Daily Allowance (RDA), which has been set according to the Food and Nutrition Board of the U.S. National Academy of Sciences to adequately meet the needs of practically all healthy persons. However, many health professionals, including myself, believe that these base RDA levels not only have been set far too low, but also do not take into account individual biochemistry. We all need to be proactive about our nutrient intake. Through testing and other assessments, correct levels for individuals can be determined.

Reduced nutrients in the soil that grows our produce are making our health vulnerable. The same carrot that grows in the ground today does not contain nearly the same amount of nutrients as a carrot grown 100 years ago due to present day pollution, over-farming, and the use of pesticides and herbicides.

The Balanced Meal

....

Many think a balanced meal is a cookie in each hand!

The following is a merely a guide, as each person has a unique biochemistry. This type of plan can help balance blood sugar and feed the body and mind.

Protein: about 2 - 3 oz. for women per meal.

Carbohydrates: ½ - ¾ cup of dense (starchy) carbohydrates such as brown rice, squash or roasted potatoes plus 1 cup or more of light carbohydrates (green vegetables). Add a fresh green salad if desired. Raw foods at meals are beneficial for digestion.

Fats: about 1 - 2 tsp. of olive oil, or a handful of nuts or seeds, or a pat of butter.

The margarine and butter wars still wage. However, even margarines that do not contain unhealthy and potentially dangerous trans-fatty acids have still been heated to high temperatures and processed for a longer shelf life. Margarine is a manufactured invention of the 20th century and is a processed fat. Pure churned butter has been used safely for thousands of years. Actually, small amounts of butter help boost your body's own GABA (another neurotransmitter) which relaxes the brain. Even Health Canada promotes that 10% of our daily fat intake be saturated.

SAMPLE MIND MEAL

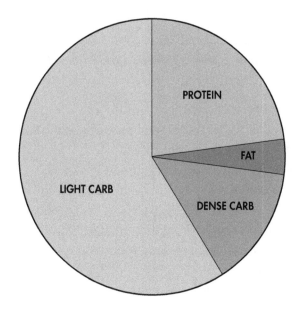

Sample Mind Meal: Adapted from "The Diet Cure Plate",
Pg. 303, *The Diet Cure*, Julia Ross. M.A.

Eating three meals a day as outlined above, plus one or two
healthful snacks will keep you fueled all day and you won't
be as tempted to gorge.

Super-Sized Servings

Many folks believe in getting their money's worth. They don't
even notice or stop eating when they are full. Animals usually eat what they need and no more. Do you often indulge in
buffets? I've never seen anyone (including myself) eat correct
portions for healthy living at buffet restaurants (or for that
matter at large family dinners!).

Do you eat too much food, too many calories? Sitting at a

dining room table for lengthy periods will encourage overeating. Most women can't or don't want to look at their reasons for excess eating; many are emotional eaters. Food is often equated with love, which causes some of us to 'self-soothe' through food. Notice if you are eating when you are full and start asking yourself why you are doing it.

Realize that fast food is very addictive.

Perfect snacks for the Frazzled Woman:
(Among other factors, an individual's weight and activity level will determine daily snacking limits—from 1 to 3 choices from the following list.)

- A piece of fruit and a handful of nuts.
- One cup of plain yogurt with some berries and a few nuts or seeds.
- An ounce of cheese and a few whole grain crackers or a piece of fruit.
- One small apple with 1 tbsp. peanut butter or almond butter.
- One cup of strawberries or watermelon and 1 kiwi and 1 slice of cheese (low fat).
- Ten medium Greek olives or 16 large green olives and 2 raw carrots.
- ¼ - ½ of an avocado spread on whole grain toast.
- One hard boiled egg and 1 cup blueberries, or ½ cantaloupe or 1 cup of pineapple.

You can try eating fruit alone between meals as a snack if you're trying to improve your digestion. Sometimes fruit and protein as suggested in the list above can be difficult for those with very poor digestion. For those with blood sugar rushes or hypoglycemia, eating fruit with nuts or a small piece of cheese is recommended to stabilize blood sugar.

Many people think that a little ice cream or cake can't hurt. And they may be right; a little won't likely be harmful now and again. However, one donut, a piece of cake or a scoop of ice cream can top up the calories and deliver the wrong kind of nutrients for the body. Obesity due to super-sized portions of fast food has become an epidemic in North America. Low quality, fatty foods steal your energy, cause weight gain and increase your risk of cancer and diabetes, not to mention (but I will) cause cholesterol levels to go through the roof which can lead to heart disease. Endangered health can trigger fear, anxiety, disability and grief. Loss of self-esteem can follow.

Too much junk food equals stress—big time.

But candy gives me energy! Betty loves chocolates, soft drinks (soda) and can't get enough of either. The pleasure center of her brain is addicted to the sugar hit. Because refined sugars offer zero vitamins or minerals, they are often referred to as 'empty calories' and the wrong kind of fuel for your brain. They offer no staying power. Frazzled Women routinely satisfy their hunger with empty calories in candy, chips and white bagels, not thinking about the weak nourishment factor in these 'filler' foods.

Empty calories = an empty brain.

Excess sugar also leads to mood swings. Betty's blood sugar rises and the hormone insulin, along with other stabilizing hormones, starts flooding the cells to try to normalize the blood sugar. If her system overcompensates and blood sugar dips too low, then Betty becomes shaky. Likely she'll instinctively reach for another cookie to drive her blood sugar back up. And up it goes again...then down it crashes. This blood sugar roller coaster ride not only leads to mood swings, but also to decreased pancreatic function—hypoglycemia and diabetes.

Sugar and alcohol are kissing cousins.

"Sugar and alcohol are both carbohydrates. Sugar addiction is directly related to alcohol addiction since sugar sensitivity is so closely linked to the metabolic pathways of alcoholism. Both sugar and alcohol evoke a beta endorphin (brain chemical) response. They dull pain, causing you to feel better for a short while. Your attachment to sugars sets you up biochemically for the addictive use of alcohol and even certain drugs."[10]

That tub of ice cream (or third glass of wine) gives the body and brain a 'buzz' as it's going down. But watch out afterwards: you might feel tired, anxious and depressed and need another sweet snack (or nightcap) to pick you up again.

Some medical authorities refute the sugar/buzz connection. Yet, have you ever observed the behavior of children the morning after Halloween? Ask any teacher what the class is like that day. The kids are often exhausted and unruly due to the highs and lows of the previous day's sugar rush and balancing act that the body endures.

It takes a lot of energy to digest food. If you eat healthy foods, the body replenishes vitamins, minerals and other

10   K. DesMaisons, Ph.D., *Potatoes Not Prozac*, Simon & Schuster, 1998, p.30

nutrients for all its efforts; if it gets refined sugar found in the form of candy bars, carbonated drinks and sweetened juices, your energy will be boosted for about half an hour. Then it's down in the dumps for you and you're looking for another sugary snack to get it back up again. The cycle continues.

Eat small amounts of protein every few hours to help break sugar cravings. Excess sugar lowers your immune system and can cause cholesterol problems and diabetes. Most North Americans eat 125-150 lbs. of sugar per year (At the turn of the last century, we ate 6 lbs. per year). Is it any wonder that our bodies can't cope?

Reduce sugar and you'll reduce stress!

Since illness is one of the greatest stressors we face, the following list will provide important links between poor diet and its unhappy by-products—stress and sickness.

Linkages Between Nutrition and Stress:

- Excess alcohol intake may damage the liver and brain. It can cause addictions, malnutrition, emotional dependence and impaired judgment – all stress producing. (Note: small amounts of red wine are recommended for heart health.)
- Sympathomimetic agents (excess caffeine, food colouring and preservatives) stimulate the stress response by activating the sympathetic nervous system.
- "High salt consumption, especially in salt sensitive individuals, increases chances of high blood pressure. And the higher the blood pressure, the more reactive blood pressure will be during stressful periods."[11]

11 W. Schafer, *Stress Management for Wellness*, 2nd Edition, Holt, Rinehart and Winston, 1992, p. 274

(Note: if you do not have high blood pressure, switch to small amounts of coarse sea salt with all the vitamins and minerals intact.)

- Excess carbohydrates set up cravings for more carbohydrates and cause weight gain. Too many carbohydrates can be responsible for high levels of blood fat called triglycerides, thereby raising the overall cholesterol count. (Weight gain and high cholesterol are both stress producing.)

- Eating excess carbohydrates and sugar (and poor quality fats) at meals can also lead to dysglycemia—disturbed blood sugar regulation, either too high (hyperglycemia) or too low (hypoglycemia). Eventually diabetes can result from repeatedly disturbed blood sugar regulation. Significant, rapid decreases in blood sugar to the brain cause shakiness, anxiety and, if not corrected immediately, can lead to more serious illnesses.

- Excess junk food robs energy. The body becomes exhausted digesting foods that give little or no nourishment in return for all its work.

- Trans fats and excessive polyunsaturated (Omega 6) fats from fast food and over-processed oils get stored in the body in the places where Omega 3 and unsaturated fats should be for optimum mental and physical functioning. The result: poor memory, lack of concentration, bad moods, aches and pains and high cholesterol.

- Emotional or physical stress in itself can cause vitamin deficiencies, such as Vitamin C and the B Vitamins. Minerals can be diminished as overstress interferes with the absorption of calcium and increases excretion of calcium, potassium, zinc, copper and magnesium. Low intakes of these minerals can also lead to osteoporosis. (In turn osteoporosis and its accompanying worry about brittle bones create a significant source of stress.)

Frazzled Woman, if you have some or even many of the above symptoms, don't despair! The body has wonderful regenerative powers. However, it's time to get back to basics with a healthy, yet filling and delicious food plan.

Begin to think about nourishing your neurotransmitters and your body at the same time, using whole foods: vegetables, fruit, low fat proteins, healthy oils and other fats, and whole grains. You'll be amazed at how favorably your brain and body will respond when you give it the vitamins, minerals, amino acids, essential fats and other nutrients it needs. Stress levels will lower as your body becomes healthier and stronger.

Don't forget to drink at least six to eight glasses of pure water daily to prevent constipation and wash toxins out of your body!

Take-Away Gems

- Recognize that your mood and stress levels can be affected by food choices.
- Balance your meals with protein, carbohydrates and fats to protect energy.
- Choose healthy natural foods instead of 'empty' calories.
- Reduce sugar to reduce stress and to maintain good mental and physical health.
- Don't skip meals.
- Stop eating when you're full.
- Drink water.

You're already tasting new health and strength. There's no better time than now to move from just surviving to really thriving.

CHAPTER EIGHT

Liberated From the Kitchen
To Fast Food Paradise . . . or Hell?

Everyone loves watching the food channels on T.V. Does anyone make any of the recipes offered? We write them down and have great intentions to follow through, but unfortunately, we're seduced by convenience and often opt for fast food. It takes time and effort to plan meals, shop for ingredients, chop vegetables, cook and clean up! Often the tired, overburdened Frazzled Woman will say, "Let's just order a pizza!"

I'm not suggesting hosting lavish dinner parties every night. However, every woman knows the warmth experienced with friends and family around the dinner table. The kitchen has been women's domain for as long as recorded time. So why have we stopped cooking? Most say it's lack of time, but likely there are many reasons.

Perhaps we're rebelling. Maybe we feel we've liberated ourselves away from the drudgery of housework, which includes cooking. It's considered 'cool' to dine in restaurants for birthdays, meetings or for friendly chats rather than at our homes. Perhaps cooking is too much tied to 'women's work' and in an era of women committed to their careers, making nutritious home-cooked meals is not seen as valuable anymore. The Frazzled Woman has risen above the lowly status of juggling pots and pans.

I'm asking you to challenge that assumption.

With the backlash of fast food on our expanding waistlines and deteriorating health, consider that cooking nutritious meals can be rewarding for your whole family. Think of yourself as a role model and revive the tradition of bringing people together for family occasions, pot luck dinners and for tea and sympathy. Preparing meals doesn't have to be seen as drudgery; it can be pleasurable. There are many ways to quickly prepare tasty and nutritious meals. Tantalizing aromas filling the kitchen are as basic as love, and truly can be an important part of your life. The old adage 'The way to a man's heart is through his stomach' still applies. Ask any guy.

At one time, I hardly turned on the stove. The refrigerator was often filled with ready-made meals. My old tried and true recipes faded into memory while I ran from store to store finding suitable meals to take home and slap down on the table after a busy day. There was this little voice nagging me, telling me it would feel more like 'home' if something were cooking in the oven or on the stove top. But I was tired, overwhelmed and cooking was the last thing on my mind. Does it bother you if you don't want to cook anymore? Not to worry. Frazzled Woman, you can feel powerful in the kitchen once again.

Preparing your own meals doesn't have to add to burnout. It may even prevent it! In your heart, you know that low fat, frozen, packaged, portioned, prepared meals do not begin to measure up to homemade fare.

How Does Your Diet Rate?

Do you sometimes feel you have brain fog after you eat? Do you get up in the morning feeling tired even though you've slept all night? Do you find yourself getting anxious a few hours after you've skipped lunch or after a meal with high sugar content? If so, your lack of attention to food choices may be adversely affecting your mental health and supporting the Frazzled Woman syndrome. Take the food and mood quiz to see how your diet rates, and then read on to discover its effects on your mood.

In this chapter you will have the opportunity to assess the contents of your pantry and your food intake, and you'll learn how to shop for foods that nourish the brain and body. In doing so, not only will you boost brain health but also help prevent hypoglycemia, stress and disease.

Food and Mood Quiz

Scoring: Give yourself one point each time you answer TRUE.

1. You eat high sugar foods every day.
2. You eat white (wheat) bread most often.
3. You mostly choose vegetables that are starchy, like potatoes and corn.
4. You eat a lot of fast food, mostly fried foods.

5. You eat a lot of packaged foods with additives or many canned foods.
6. When asked what vegetables you eat the most, you would answer," Fries."
7. You drink 3 to 8 cups of coffee a day.
8. You seldom drink water during the day.
9. You drink alcohol every day—the equivalent of more than 2 glasses of wine.
10. You skip meals, especially breakfast and sometimes lunch as well.
11. You never or seldom eat fish.
12. You live on soda or diet drinks (more than three per day).
13. You have extreme cravings for certain foods: milk, pasta, cheese, cereals, bread, apple juice or orange juice.

If your score is:

1 - 5 You try to eat healthfully but sometimes slip up. Work on the points to which you answered TRUE for better clarity of the mind.

6 - 9 You don't give much thought about what you eat. At times, you feel anxious or depressed and don't know why. Start to attend to the quality of your diet to feed your brain.

10 - 13 You have many cravings and 'brain fog.' You have trouble remembering things and sometimes get panic attacks and/or depression. Start to choose a healthier, natural diet.

Take control of the foods you eat. The modern day Frazzled Woman is busy and often looks for ways to save time on preparation of meals. While saving time is the goal, the consequences can be serious if she makes the wrong choices.

Where do we eat our meals? A large percentage of people eat in restaurants for many meals. We eat in our cars, in airplanes, or on other forms of public transportation. Sometimes we even eat at home.

Do your choices make you feel energized? Do you have good digestion? Or do you have heartburn, indigestion, constipation, and/or diarrhea? If you constantly suffer from headaches, fatigue, lack of energy and health problems, instead of looking at your diet last, why not look at it **first**?

How many of these 'natural' engineered foods do you eat?

Check your ingredient labels.

- Peanut Butter with added icing sugar and hydrogenated oil
- Ketchup laced with sugar
- Soy sauce made with caramel, sugar and salt
- Turkey roll or other processed meats, made with salt, sugar and chemicals
- Highly heated oil-based products such as cooking oils, salad dressings, and mayonnaise (oils are heated to very high temperatures to assure a long shelf life—unless the bottle says 'cold pressed')
- Items containing aspartame: soda, desserts, yogurt, sweeteners
- Junk food snacks: potato chips, pretzels, licorice, chocolate bars
- White flour products: pizza, cakes, pastries, waffles, pancakes, crackers, bread
- Processed cheese
- 'Energy' bars containing large portions of sugar
- Processed whipped cream or other toppings substituting cream with chemicals

If most of the foods you eat are found in the above list and you don't feel well, it's time to switch to other brands or other products.

We consume too much salt. All animals, including humans need salt (sodium chloride). Cows are given 'salt licks' so that they can take what they need. Nonetheless, we regularly ingest an excess of this seasoning, especially in fast foods, packaged processed foods, canned goods and meals made outside of the home. Foods high in sodium include snack foods such as crackers, nachos, potato chips and pretzels, cheese, gravies and sauces, processed luncheon meats, canned or dried soups and frozen meals.

Every health guide recommends that we use less table salt because sodium can contribute to increasing the risk for high blood pressure.

For centuries, small amounts of sea salt or Himalayan natural salt have been considered beneficial since they contain many other healthful minerals; however, for some people with high blood pressure, even these preferred salts may have to be limited.

There are healthy substitutes for processed foods. Your body will appreciate pure natural peanut and other nut butters such as almond, cashew or sesame butter. Ketchup is available with a healthier form of sugar and less of it. Natural soy sauce without additives can be found in your grocery store, often under the name tamari sauce or Bragg, All Purpose Liquid Soy Seasoning. Processed turkey rolls are not the best protein choice with their added sugar, salt and preservatives. Choose instead nitrate-free processed meats or better yet, roast your own turkey at home. Try bottled salad dressings with more natural ingredients, or use pure olive oil with vinegar or lemon juice.

In 1994, the Department of Health and Human Services released a list of 61 reported adverse reactions to aspartame, including chest pains, asthma, arthritis, migraine headaches, insomnia, seizures, tremors, vertigo, and weight gain. Instead of diet soda (which contains aspartame), drink water (with a twist of lime or lemon) or mineral water. Eat fresh fruit instead of desserts containing aspartame. Buy plain yogurt and add fresh fruits, or jams sweetened with only natural juices.

When you're snacking or preparing desserts, make a habit of reading labels for chemical contents. Seek out healthy treats such as bars containing nuts, seeds and dried fruit, or indulge in a small amount of dark chocolate (containing over 70% cocoa). Use real (low fat) cow's milk, goat or sheep milk cheese instead of processed, 'plastic' cheese. If you occasionally must have whipped cream, use the real product instead of whipped chemicals.

Back to Basics

From the beginning of time, food has been used to nourish mind and body in order for us to survive and thrive. Bodies need proteins, complex carbohydrates, essential fatty acids and water to ensure a steady supply of vitamins, minerals and other essential nutrients. The mitochondria, found within the cytoplasm of each cell, are important to cellular respiration, but they need energy to provide their special power

Many people express the attitude, "If it's not good for us, **they** wouldn't be allowed to sell it." I wish that statement were true. Many 'foods' on your grocery shelf and in take-out restaurants contain sugar, salt and chemicals—added for taste and shelf life. According to Health Canada, the U.S. Department of Health and Human Services, the Heart and Stroke Foundation of Canada, the American Heart Association, and the American and Canadian Cancer Societies, we need to limit these items for better health.

Take charge of your dietary choices instead
of leaving them to food processing companies
and fast food restaurants to decide for you.

Many children and adults alike are making steady diets of non-foods. People get hooked on the taste of packaged snacks; but then they're dealing with powerful addictions which are difficult to break. More than that, the body and brain don't know what to do with all these engineered chemicals and fats. You get filled up and there's no room left for other good nutrients such as fruits and vegetables, our antioxidant champs.

Research shows that antioxidants are powerful substances that help protect us from disease and give us vitality.

Author and psychiatrist Abram Hoffer, MD, PhD says "Of the thousands of items in our grocery stores, about fifty would be suitable for human health." What are those fifty? They are those items found around the perimeters of your grocery store such as fruits and vegetables, meats, low fat dairy, eggs and whole grain products.

We feed our pets high quality diets
for good health and ignore ourselves.

Become a prudent shopper and choose better quality items that are free of additives. Many companies are acting responsibly and take seriously information being released about damaging hydrogenated fats, high sugar and salt as additives in products and their negative effects on our health. Market-savvy food companies now produce better products to sustain and enhance our health rather than ruin it. I applaud them.

Some grocery stores have sections for Natural or Health Foods. If you can afford organic products, buy them. They lower the load of chemicals entering your body. I challenge you to make wise choices for products that feed your mind and shape up your body.

Are these healthy products expensive? No.

- Bags of brown rice
- Natural oatmeal
- Frozen (or fresh) vegetables grown locally
- Apples and pears
- Air popped popcorn
- Plain yogurt
- Cans of tuna or salmon
- Frozen fish
- Chicken

What's your health worth anyway? Ask someone who doesn't have good health.

What Else Can You Eat? Lots.

Choose a variety of foods to ensure an optimum range of vitamins and minerals:

- Whole grain products: wheat, spelt, whole rye, brown rice breads, cereals, breads, crackers or pastas (in moderation). (Bloating, diarrhea or constipation can be a sign of allergies or sensitivities to certain grains.)
- Proteins such as fish, chicken, lamb, beef, turkey, yogurt, low fat cheeses, soy products and eggs.
- An array of plant foods: vegetables, fruits, nuts, seeds, legumes, beans.
- Good fats: olive oil, canola oil, butter, olives, avocados, natural peanut or almond butter, butter. Only small amounts are necessary.

Add fish to your diet. The Omega 3 fats in fish and fish oil supplements are good for your brain and heart. Research shows that people in countries where more fish is consumed have fewer incidences of depression, bipolar disorder and post-natal depression.[12] Just watch out for fish high in mercury. According to the U.S. FDA advisory, nearly all fish contains trace amounts of methylmercury, which is not harmful to humans. However, long-lived, larger fish that feed on other fish accumulate the highest levels of methylmercury and pose the greatest risk to people who eat them regularly. Protect yourself (especially if you are pregnant or a nursing mother) and your family by not eating these large fish that can contain high levels of methylmercury: shark, swordfish, king mackerel, and tilefish.

The smaller fish have the least amounts of mercury. You can safely eat 12 ounces per week of cooked fish. A typical single serving size of fish is from 3 to 6 ounces. Of course, if your serving sizes are smaller, you can eat fish more frequently. You can choose shellfish, canned fish, smaller ocean fish or farm-raised fish. Just pick a variety of different species.[13]

Brush on a little olive oil, sprinkle on some herbs and broil or grill for a fast protein choice that will perk up your brain.

Olive oil is the key ingredient in the Mediterranean diet. In the last few years, this diet has caught the attention of doctors, nutritionists and researchers all over the world because the Mediterranean countries tend to have some of the healthiest people. They boast some of the highest life expectancies

---

12 Hibbeln, 1998, Tanskanen et al, 2001, Archives of General Psychiatry, 58, 512-513

13 *AHA Scientific Statement: Fish Consumption, Fish Oil, Omega-3 Fatty Acids, and Cardiovascular Disease* Penny M. Kris-Etherton, PhD, RD; William S. Harris, PhD; Lawrence J. Appel, MD, MPH, for the Nutrition Committee

compared to many of the more economically well-developed countries of Northern Europe.

The Mediterranean Diet was first presented academically by Dr. Walter Willett of the School of Public Health at Harvard University. In the mid-1990's, Willett examined the diet and food patterns of people living in Crete, Greece and southern Italy and laid out the common aspects of those diets along with the apparent benefits of the diet.[14]

But what makes this most interesting is that despite the guidelines stating that dietary fat should be kept down to about 30% of our daily calorie intake, for people who live in the Mediterranean countries (Greece for example), fat makes up 40% or more of the daily diet. But it's the type of fat that makes all the difference—**olive oil**.

Olive oil, the primary source of fat in the Mediterranean diet, has been making headlines, and for good reason. It seems this bitter little fruit produces oil that is rich in healthy antioxidant tocopherols, carotenoids, polyphenols and the omega 9 fatty acid, oleic acid.

Among its many claims, preliminary studies show that olive oil can:
- help manage healthy cholesterol levels and LDL oxidation
- control healthy blood clotting and circulation
- help scavenge dangerous free radicals
- support healthy blood pressure levels

Make sure pure olive oil or a high quality omega 3, 6 and 9 fish oil capsules are part of your diet.

14 Willett W.C. (01 June 1995), "Mediterranean diet pyramid: a cultural model for healthy eating", *American Journal of Clinical Nutrition* 61 (6): 1402S-6S. PMID 7754995

Too busy to cook? Cook in batches and freeze protein choices (e.g. chicken, meat balls or patties made from ground chicken or turkey or beef or salmon). Use a grill, such as a Foreman or Hamilton Beach for fast, easy, low-fat cooking. While the chicken breasts or pieces of fish grill, you can steam some vegetables (in minutes) and put sweet potatoes in the microwave oven. I'm not a large fan of microwaves but use them occasionally when pressed for time. If you're really on the run, buy a BBQ chicken and make the sides when you get home. Slow-cookers are enormous time savers. In the morning, put ingredients in the cooker before work and arrive home to a cooked, prepared meal. Healthy ingredients such as chicken, chunks of fish or meat or beans with some frozen vegetables, cut up potatoes, a can of tomatoes, and spices will provide a filling and delicious meal. Slow cookers are ideal to use for chili con carne.

Frozen vegetables are handy to store in your freezer and can be prepared in minutes. Keep greens in your fridge in breathable plastic bags specifically made for vegetables. Correctly stored, they keep for a longer time and are always ready for a quick salad. Add cucumber, tomato, some walnuts or olives, sliced carrots or peppers and you can't go wrong.

Other fast cooking ideas include whole grain pastas. Toss cooked shrimp or other sea food into the boiled and drained pasta noodles. Add pesto or any natural or organic sauce of your choice. Serve this quick and easy-to-make dish with a salad.

In the organic or natural section of some supermarkets or health food stores, you can buy ready-made soups in jars or in cartons for easy storage. Vegetable soups are a ready source of vitamins and minerals and fill you up. People who eat non-creamed soup as a first course don't generally eat as much at meals and can help keep their weight in check. Some of the dehydrated vegetable soups (organic section) in small individual servings are good for travelling or as an addition to a meal. Make sure the label indicates the product is low in sodium.

Healthy Choices in Restaurants

Do you make meals or reservations? Eating in restaurants can seem like a saving grace for the Frazzled Woman. However many establishments, especially several of the large chain restaurants use products heavy with trans-fatty acids, sodium and sugar. Young children are already being diagnosed with early diabetes, and the incidence of cholesterol problems and obesity for young adults is on the rise because of too many fast foods. Even if a woman doesn't think of her own health, I can bet that she doesn't want her children to suffer.

Many restaurants offer heart healthy choices with less fat, sugar, or salt than other selections. Look for these on menus. Watch out though for buffets. Try not to gorge. Fill your plate with lots of green vegetables and use dressing sparingly. Select a piece of protein (e.g. fish, or chicken that isn't deep-fried), add some rice (not half your plateful) and head to the fresh fruit section for dessert.

Buffets notoriously feature a lot of starchy foods such as mashed potatoes with gravy, corn on the cob, and rice pudding. These high starch foods along with tall glasses of soda are culprits for weight gain and high cholesterol.

If you must eat fast food, order a plain burger without the cheese, bacon and mayo. If you order chicken in fast food restaurants, order roast chicken, not fried. Resist the fries if you can (or have a small amount) and order a salad. If you order pizza, add a salad, or a piece of fruit. Order a slice or two instead of a whole pizza for yourself. Better yet stay away from fast food restaurants. Home-cooking style restaurants are often your best bet.

If you're constantly on the road, carry healthy snacks. Nuts, dried fruit, yogurt, banana, healthy power bars with seeds in them, small cans of fish with zip-off tops, carrot slices or sticks, and raw snap peas are good choices.

Eating at parties can be disastrous to the waistline. Cocktail parties? Eat the shrimp, chick peas, sushi, a couple of pieces of cheese and crackers, and steer clear of the breaded, deep fried hors d'oeuvres or small quiches. Dessert? Fruit is always the best choice, but you could just eat a small piece of cake or a few spoonfuls of dessert. Don't let others push food on you. Suggested replies to someone who wants you to taste everything: "Thanks, but I'm really quite satisfied," or "Everything was so good, but I can't eat another bite," or "I'd love to, but I have food allergies."

What Else Causes Brain Fog and Affects Mood?

You may have food allergies. If you can afford organic products, go for it! They lower the load of chemicals entering your body through pesticides and herbicides. It is especially important to use organic dairy products, since pesticides tend to accumulate in the fat of an animal. Pesticides reside in the fat tissues in our bodies and in our brains which, incidentally, are largely made up of fat tissue. As for beef, grass-fed beef is best. Again, if you can afford other organic meats, poultry and eggs, you can protect your health. Wild fish is best along with organically-raised farmed fish.

"There are innumerable reasons why some children, occasionally or frequently, appear to be unable to learn or suddenly act inappropriately in class. Sometimes these changes can be related directly to foods which have been eaten or exposure to chemical odors or common allergenic substances."[15] Dr. Doris Rapp, who specializes in food allergies and children's behavioural problems, emphasizes that any child or adult can manifest the identical changes such as red earlobes, dark blue, black or red eye circles or red rouge-like cheek patches (and many more physical or behavioral symptoms) due to unusual reactions to various foods or chemicals in our environment.

In the *Annals of Allergy*, 1982, it was reported that 100% of the depressed patients tested were allergic to egg whites. Some had additional allergies to cereals, grains and milk. According to Toronto allergist, Bernard Zylberberg MD, when your mood is low or frenetic or when you struggle to remember something, you might consider that you may not be optimally nourished. Your thinking, feeling, mental energy and focus happen across a network of interconnecting brain cells, each one of which depends on an optimal supply of nutrients in order to work efficiently.

Mold and ragweed are two environmental allergens that are associated with food problems and that includes anything that has been fermented or uses the yeast process: wines, beer, vinegar, soy sauce and breads with yeast. Also, according to Dr. Zylberberg, nightshade vegetables (tomatoes, potatoes, eggplant and peppers) can be highly allergenic.

Some laboratories conduct ELISA blood testing for IgG antibody levels for those foods that give delayed sensitivity reactions up to 48 hours after eating a food. IgE allergic reactions are those that occur within a few hours after contact with offending foods or inhalants.

You may start feeling better after avoiding the offending foods for one to six weeks. Keeping a food and mood diary over a period of time may be a good way to track food allergies.

---

15 D. J. Rapp, M.D., FAAA, FAAP, *The Impossible Child*, Practical Allergy Research Foundation, p.3

Take-Away Food Gems

- Consider cooking more often for yourself and your family.
- Avoid sugar and refined foods. Refined foods are processed foods. The more refined and processed a food, the less nutritious it becomes. For example: brown rice is a whole natural food. White rice is a processed food; the outer grain has been stripped away along with the vitamins, minerals and healthy oils. Governments often demand that companies re-infuse nutrients to these processed foods, but usually only a fraction of what was taken out. The result—a food lacking in essential nutrients. If this pattern of eating processed food choices is repeated often, a person's health can be compromised.[16]
- Include small amounts of protein at each meal (animal or vegetarian sources).
- Eat more vegetables, fresh fruit, and whole foods (e.g. seeds, nuts, beans, lentils, whole grains). Include vegetables at lunch and dinner. Soup counts.
- Have a heaping tablespoon of ground seeds (sesame, sunflower, pumpkin, flax), or a tablespoon of their oil every day. Fish oil for a higher amount of EPA to DHA is recommended.[17]
- If your diet contains a lot of wheat, experiment for two weeks without it, substituting rice, buckwheat (kasha), corn or oats instead. Note that continued symptoms of chronic fatigue, bloating, indigestion and/or abdominal pain require a physician's diagnosis for possible food

16 Carpenter, Kenneth J, *Beriberi, White Rice, and Vitamin B: A Disease, A Cause, and A Cure*, University of California Press 2000, p. 282
17 Peet & Horrobin, 2001, Tanskanen et al, 2001, *Journal of Psychopharmacology*, 15 (suppl.), A12

allergies, including gluten intolerance, requiring diet-specific treatment.

- If your diet contains a lot of milk products (milk, cheese, yogurt etc.) experiment for two weeks by eliminating them, using soy or almond milk instead. Lactose (milk sugar) intolerance causes gastric distress for some people, and may require a switch to lactose-free dairy. Some people may be allergic to the milk protein itself and even lactose-free dairy would not make a difference to their gastric distress symptoms. Many people can tolerate goat or sheep milk products while still being allergic to cow's milk products. It's best to be tested by your health professional to make sure.
- Don't let more than four to five hours go by without eating.
- Drink 6–8 glasses of water each day.
- Ensure an optimal intake of vitamins, minerals and essential fats.
- Reduce or avoid stimulants, namely tea, coffee, chocolate, cola drinks, cigarettes.
- Reduce or avoid alcohol. Drinking alcohol increases your allergic potential.
- Avoid unnecessary stress as it affects digestion.

Track Your Food

In your notebook, set aside 7 pages as a Food Diary. On each page, down the left hand side, list your meals and snacks for each day for the next week. Leave enough spaces in order to fill in your food choices for each of the following: Breakfast, Lunch, Snack, Dinner, Snack. Track your food choices to bring you into reality about what goes into your mouth each day.

Review your summary at the end of the first week and see what you can substitute for any poor food choices for the second week. Plan ahead for simple yet healthful meals and snacks. Try to make food preparation and cooking a family activity. Don't know how to cook? Ask friends for recipes, download recipes from the Internet, or watch the Food Channel on TV. Go to the library and find a cookbook to cater to your tastes and need to eat wholesome foods. Many great cookbooks are available on the market. Start somewhere.

If you used to cook and have recently used your stove elements as a surface to display plants, see if you can bring the art of preparing and cooking meals back into your home. But more importantly, remember why you stopped cooking. Enlist family help or approach your cooking from a new perspective. Invest in better cooking utensils and some friendly cookbooks.

Looking after your nutritional needs is basic and vital to ensure high energy, low stress, smooth, clear, healthy-looking skin, teeth and nails. Your immune system will love you for it and you'll have fewer sick days. Change takes time. It's okay to alter habits gradually. What's also fantastic about using good nutrition is that your weight will also normalize naturally. You'll look and feel great.

Bonus: Are you walking, moving, stretching, dancing, gardening or doing exercises? (Your prize is that you'll burn calories and raise your immunity!)

Goodbye Frazzled Woman.
Hello Healthy, Beautiful, Powerful Woman!

CHAPTER NINE

Time Flies . . .
How to Catch It

The Frazzled Woman is an expert at rushing. She is able to squeeze 20 tasks into 10 minutes including putting on lipstick in the rear-view mirror of her car while driving. (She's had car accidents more than once because of this!) If she's really adept, a cup of coffee teeters in one hand. She snacks while driving and has been known to text messages at red lights (or while driving). At day's end, with her briefcase slung over one shoulder, her stomach in a knot and her arms on fire, she'll manage to juggle bags of groceries, then carry on to pick up children at day care.

Everything that she set out to do in a day has been accomplished—well, almost everything. Her mind is jumping from one idea to the next. Her heart pounds. She has a nagging feeling that she forgot something. After flopping into bed, she awakens in a startled sweat at 3:00 a.m. because she realizes she forgot to pick up an important document from a colleague for a work-related project due in the morning! When the alarm clock rings at 6:00 a.m. the next day, the rush with all its problem-solving and frenzy begins again. Time seems to be slipping into the future. Sound familiar?

A Moment
I grab this moment
as it passes by
so fleeting, but yet
so satisfying
while it lasts.
Wanting escape,
it playfully bounces
through my fingers
and I grasp it
even tighter.
Its aura surrounds me,
encases me with warmth,
acceptance, and I savor
its sweet taste in my mouth
and feel its soft velvet
on my skin.

The pure joy of this moment
clears and calms my mind.
I want to laugh, caress, love . . .
   but then it's gone,
   floating into eternity,
   enduring as a
   precious memory
   in my heart and
   in my mind.

by Rosalie Moscoe

It's 1998. I'm at my computer completely engrossed, preparing a time management seminar for a client. The work is interesting, but my neck and back are aching. I'm anxious to finish and look forward to the therapeutic massage I booked for later in the day.

The phone rings. I quickly pick it up and the voice on the other end says, "Rosalie, this is Joanne, your massage therapist. You're a half hour late for your appointment. Is there something wrong?" Embarrassed, I could feel the blood rushing to my face. "Oh no," I answer, "I'm working on a time management seminar and . . . I lost track of the time." We both break into hysterical laughter. I was lucky. She didn't even charge me for the missed appointment. Not all missed appointments result in laughter.

But I've come to believe that mistakes are really lessons to be learned. And these mistakes can be used as a springboard toward a successful way to live and to renew our future.

> *"The bad news is, time flies.*
> *The good news is, you're the pilot."*
> — *Michael Althsuler*

So what kind of pilot are you? In control or going down?

Right now, I want you to just relax. All new behaviors start with a thought, idea, or a picture in your mind. I'm going to invite you to imagine yourself managing your time well. Everything is running smoothly, work gets done, your home is in order and dinner has been planned. You're not stressed. You are the time manager of your dreams.

If you want, you can close your eyes and imagine it. Think about how you feel. In your mind's eye, notice that you appear happy and relaxed while you work. You have just set positive thoughts into action. Keep them as you read this chapter.

Today, we have more time-saving devices at home and in offices than ever before in history, yet have you ever noticed that most of us have **no time**? In Matthew Fox's book, *The Reinvention of Work*, he reports that since the dawning of the Industrial Revolution, we have a need to be like the machine: to work faster and faster, to fill every hour, every minute with work. But it's not only work that's the culprit, it's the act of stuffing every minute with **something**. Women seem to feel they're wasting time if they're not on the phone, working, shopping, or cooking. To put one's feet up and read a book or watch a movie has become a forgotten pleasure for many.

A machine, a computer, may be able
to work 24 hours a day. A person cannot.

Striking a balance is an important part of managing your time: taking time for your family, your friends, your community, your own health. You're thinking, "I have no time for those things." Then where is your time going?

Are you taking on too much or are you wasting your time? Only you know what's too much for you. To fill every minute with work would be a mistake. During the course of the day, we need a break by taking a walk around the block or enjoying a chat or joke with a friend or colleague.

Multi-tasking to save time is a myth. You're only rattling your brain! You might think you are saving time, but in the end, you're only creating chaos in your mind. You can only process one thought at a time. You may think you can do more, but in actuality your thoughts are flipping back and forth from one thing to another in nanoseconds.

If you talk to someone on the phone at the same time as you're composing an e-mail, your attention to the person on the phone is half-hearted. The message you write will likely have mistakes, and you will have failed on both counts! We all do it, but it would be better to be working towards the higher goal of being in the moment. Have a shorter phone call and resume e-mailing afterwards.

Women are famous for doing more than one thing at a time. In the past, I would have mopped the floor, thrown in a load of laundry and wiped a counter during the course of a casual phone call with a friend. While there's no real danger of becoming too distracted, I realize now that I wasn't fully with my friends on those calls. Many women may do this mindless multi-tasking even if it's an intense personal call or one that is work-related. The problem is that your concentration and focus become 'fuzzy' along with the quality of your responses. Reduced productivity or strained relationships can be the result.

The examples in the opening paragraph in this chapter about distractions while driving can result in wrapping your car around a hydro pole in seconds flat. (In your heart, you already know that.) On a subconscious level, recklessness becomes a thrill. You're likely an 'adrenaline junkie' if you enjoy the kind of feats that test Fate.

It would be better to learn the skill of skydiving and enjoy the adventure of the moment that way than to live on the edge each day or even each moment of your life. At least while skydiving, the thrill is experienced in a controlled atmosphere with safety mechanisms in place. I know someone who drives using her leg on the steering wheel while eating something with one hand and talking on the phone with the other—no safety mechanisms there! Obviously for some, that kind of activity can be very exciting! The reward, every time, is in getting away with it without consequences.

The Adrenaline Junkie

It's the high a person feels when gambling—the thrill of an adrenaline rush while waiting for the right card or for the right number to come up—the thrill of the almost win or a chance to win. Some people love the emotional high or get addicted to it. Like any addiction, it can be difficult to break.

Your adrenal glands (two of them, each located above your kidneys at your back) help give you energy when you need it. When the stress response kicks in and the body's metabolism speeds up, the adrenal glands pump more adrenaline into the system.

These powerful little allies in your body help to boost your metabolism in case you need to run fast to catch a subway or bus, or if you're being chased by a dog or by some unsavory character. However, by switching on our adrenal glands at every turn during the day, we're creating a burden for them. I can just hear these adrenal glands wondering, "What's the hurry? Is there a race going on all day?" Yes there is.

If you're living in the fast lane, always under the wire, and love the thrill of being busy and rushing, **almost** getting into accidents, **almost** falling flat onto the sidewalk, **almost** being late, you likely are an adrenaline junkie. Welcome to the club.

I once got a fortune cookie that said: "He who hurries loses dignity." (I assumed that referred to women as well.)

North Americans are known for their hurried habits. It's like living in emergency mode all the time when most of the time there's no real emergency. Unfortunately for you, the Frazzled Woman's way of life wears you out because the mind and body cannot cope for long with this accelerated pace. Life doesn't have to be this way. Your awareness that you are living at a heightened pace is the very first step to ultimately taming the Frazzled beast.

Want to catch time?
Instead of going faster . . . SLOW DOWN.

This is the first and most important step.

If you notice that you're rushing, immediately take a few deep breaths. If you are doing more than one thing at a time, notice it and stop doing one of the activities; it could save your life. If you feel you are walking too fast, eating too fast, take a few deep breaths and slow down your pace. Eat more slowly and chew each mouthful instead of gulping it down. During conversations, slow your pace of speaking, limit your own speaking time, and enjoy eye contact. You'll become a better listener . . .and everyone loves to be listened to.

Irrational Beliefs about Time. How Do You Rate?

If you are constantly out of time, then check your belief system. From the list of these next few statements, keep track of the number of times you answer YES:

- I must always be productive.
- I cannot delegate because no one can meet my standards.
- I must usually hurry to get everything done.
- If I spend time relaxing, resting or exercising, I will certainly fall behind in more important things.
- I cannot help but be upset or anxious until a task is complete.
- I have no control over constant overload in my life.
- I must be all things to all people.

If you answer YES more than four times, likely you feel overworked, overstressed, and you lack the control you think you have. Awareness of your own stress level is crucial to job performance and to your health.

And it's not only the workplace that could be the issue. It could be problems at home: economic issues, personal financing, or issues around elder care. Issues around children can be the real culprit. Kids can do it to you every time.

Work affects health and health affects work. Sometimes it's a tradeoff. When you spend more time at work, you may be missing spending time with your family, or missing a workout at the gym or a much needed walk around the block.

Overworking might benefit your career in the short run, but in the long term these tradeoffs can take their toll on business and one's personal life or health. Absenteeism in the workplace from stress-related illnesses is high.

Ronald J. Burke, Professor Emeritus of *Organizational Studies* and researcher at York University, Toronto has found that workaholism is a serious threat to marriages and families. Some people can't stop working, even after a job is done. For them, vacations are torments. Computers are commonly seen on planes and on the beach, while cell phones ring everywhere, even in public toilet stalls. The 'high' one feels when being productive can become an addiction.

Then again, overwork may truly mean that too much work is piled on you. Maybe you do too good a job. Everyone depends upon you. "I'll give this project to Mary; she'll do it for me." And you, Mary, always take care of it. As mentioned in an earlier chapter, you may have to learn to say NO in order to save your time from flying out the window. On the other hand, overwork can often be based in self-induced worry or a lack of self-confidence about being able to do the work on time.

Sometimes, people even overwork to avoid going home.

Whatever the problem, don't let it go unattended. If you feel you are at the breaking point, I urge you to get the help you need from a psychologist, social worker or psychiatrist before you fall victim to serious illness. Start with your doctor or other healthcare provider or religious leader of your community. If you're looking for reduced fees, ask for a referral or call a religious family service group in your area. Don't be embarrassed. They've likely heard stories similar to yours before.

Calming Computer Depression

What now? Another computer crash! Technology stress has scored again! Deadlines are approaching and critical files are nowhere to be found. What's our first reaction? Fight? Flight? Throwing a tantrum?

As a society we are dependent on computers and when we need them the most, they often decide to sabotage us. Computer crashes cause us anger, stress and a rise in cholesterol levels. We get shaky, feel tense or nauseous. The impact of technology on stress is always accelerating.

Non-functioning technical equipment can be an enormous source of anxiety, frustration and stress-related illnesses. Machines can't possibly feel remorse for their breakdowns; yet many people react emotionally when equipment quits on them.

So how can we practice stress management in the office to protect our blood pressure from soaring? The first step is to adjust our attitudes so that we can remain calm. Those who carry a great deal of responsibility in their jobs will likely feel even more pressure when computers take an unexpected break.

Five Rescue Remedies
for Computer Related Stress

1. Take a few deep breaths and think to yourself "Tomorrow the sun will rise again. I can take steps to control the situation." Positive thinking techniques can be a boon not only to your mental health but also your physical well-being. As mentioned in previous chapters, positive self-talk can be used to alleviate many stressful situations.

2. Know that you can resolve the crisis. If you cannot fix the

problem, likely your first call is to a technician who can. Most importantly, keep calm instead of letting the frustration strangle you to the point of severe anxiety.

3. Before you tackle the situation, either go for a short walk or jog around the block, pound a pillow if you think it will help or get a cup of soothing green tea! Talk to a colleague if it makes you feel better. Once you calm down, you'll be more able to form a plan to resolve the consequences of the information or time lost. Negative attitudes (screaming at technicians) will only alienate those who are there to help you.

4. While you are waiting for a technician (or inspiration) to arrive, shift your attention to another task. Organize your desk or plan for upcoming work. For anxiety relief, deep breathe. Let your hands go limp, and then shake them and do shoulder rolls to help you relax. If you cannot use your e-mail, make some phone calls—a novel idea!

5. Prevent computer depression and technology stress by making sure you have excellent backup systems. An inexpensive solution to saving important work is to use USB drive sticks. Being prepared against another crash or freeze-up may also require technical assistance to make sure your computer is updated and running properly.

Know that you are not alone in experiencing computer chaos. As I talk to friends and colleagues experiencing these all too common technology glitches, I realize we need to alter our attitudes. Like traffic jams, there's often little we can do at the moment. However, even traffic jams eventually are cleared. So, Frazzled Woman, when technology decides to halt production, cool down and know that "This too shall pass."

What Do I Need to Accomplish?
Setting Priorities

Clarifying and then setting priorities are the first two crucial steps to achieving desired results.

You may want to ask yourself "What do I want to accomplish in life? What is the most valuable use of my time?" These questions are important not only to accomplish goals, but also to use as a spiritual exercise. After all, when we start to question what it is we wish to accomplish in life, our thoughts fall into the realm of "Why am I here anyway?" I think these are good questions to ask ourselves now and again.

In your notebook or journal, title a page **Why Am I Here Anyway?** Jot down whatever comes to your mind: to enjoy life, to do my work, to help others, to be of service to others, to do God's work, to make money, to look after my family, to help my friends, to fulfill my destiny, to leave a legacy. . . there may be several answers.

If you know what it is you want to accomplish, then you'll know what it is you need to prioritize. What you want to accomplish can change over time. For example, most people in past generations stayed in the same jobs their whole lives. Today, likely due to changing technology and changing attitudes, we have more choices about careers, whether we continue to stay in them our whole lives or change midstream to one or more vocations along the way.

Today, in North America and in many countries, women have many career choices that were not open to them in past generations. Women are doctors, lab technicians, dentists, teachers, lawyers, musicians, singers, accountants, professional athletes, judges; they work in retail sales, as executive assistants or receptionists. There once was a time when, if a woman teacher married or got pregnant, she was forced to quit her job. Thankfully, times have changed. Paid maternity leave is the norm for many jobs. Some people will need to work to make money; others will need to do it for their sanity in addition to the financial rewards. Others are doing too much and need to pull back and take time for themselves by cultivating new interests or replacing the ones they find boring or unfulfilling.

To admit and verbalize your favorite goals is an important step for feeling in charge and going forward in life. Crystallizing your desires will help you spend your time more effectively.

Achievements and Wish Fulfillment

Without an eye on where we want to go, we are merely worker ants, just doing the prescribed job following the next ant in front of us. If we want to get somewhere, we'd better pick a destination or we won't arrive.

Notice whether your desires are vague or concrete. If they are vague, that might be okay for you. But to be truly successful at what you want to accomplish, you'll need to ask yourself questions: "What's important to me? Where do I want to be in a year, in five years? What do I want to accomplish for myself, for my family, for my self-development goals?" You may need time to think about this, to really ponder what it is you want out of life. Once you have some firm goals, then you can devise an action plan to convert them into a reality.

Be realistic about your goals and the steps required to achieve them. This sample planner is the next step forward following your Personal Wellness Wheel assessment found in Chapter 3. Perhaps after reading through previous chapters you're ready to make some serious plans for real life achievements.

A SAMPLE PLANNER for real life achievement

MY LIFE	WHAT I WANT TO ACHIEVE
Vocational	Pick up the credits I need to get that supervisor's job – 2 year target
Physical	Tone up – take off those pounds. Call local recreation center for their schedules – now. Cut down on junk food. Schedule my annual check-up.
Family	Sit down with family and figure out a reasonable vacation this year – we all need it! Start cleaning house to stage it for a move – next year? Clean out junk in basement.
Social	Call, write more often to friends living across the country – maybe connect with them halfway somewhere. Make time to get together with friends in town.
Financial	Consolidate debts and get the highest interest credit cards paid off. Work out a budget and a savings plan. Call bank for an appointment – this week.
Other Stress Relief	Calm myself at work. Do some deep breathing. Pack a better lunch and take a walk at lunch hour.
Spiritual	Go to religious services this week or next. Read a book on spirituality. Remind myself daily to be grateful for what I have and the people in my life.

One of these life areas will demand more thought and attention. It will present itself as a priority. Tend to it first.

Point your compass to the mark
and then start moving towards it.

This exercise gives you some thought to your direction and a plan for many areas of your life. Things change of course, but planning is your compass, pointing in the direction of how you will spend your time and with that **your life**.

You can make up a quick chart now, with long and short timelines. Use the sample chart above as your guideline. Depending on your personality, you will expand it, condense it, or convert it to a wall poster. It's up to you.

That plan is your map through the desert of indecision, procrastination and wishful thinking. Keep moving forward. If you merely just think about what you could do, your dreams remain unfulfilled. You know you need to take some action to accomplish your visions. What's stopping you?

Procrastination: The Time Robber

Sometimes we need to procrastinate in order to weigh the pros and cons if we're making large life decisions: getting married, buying a house, taking a long trip, having a child.

But often small issues left undone can drag you down; for example, cleaning out your desk. What tasks or decisions are you dragging along like a ball and chain?

Actually, procrastination is bad for your health. *Psychology Today* magazine reported that studies at Carleton University in Ottawa reveal that procrastination is part of an unhealthy lifestyle. College students who procrastinate have higher levels of drinking, smoking, insomnia, stomach problems, cold and flu.

Why Do You Procrastinate?

The main reasons for procrastination may be:
- Dislike of a project. The very thought of cleaning a cupboard makes you feel ill.
- Having to work on tasks in the evening when you're exhausted.
- Fear of failure (or success). "I'll only fail so why bother trying?" Or, "If I succeed I'll have too much responsibility."
- Half-hearted goals where you don't care about the outcome of the project.
- Perfectionism. You feel you can't start a project until you have all the information or tools at hand.

In his audio program *How to Master Your Time*, Brian Tracy says that procrastination may be a holdover from your school days when you hated to start your homework. Tracy suggests instead of an "I'll do it later" attitude, you may need to shift to a "Do it now" attitude. Use **positive self-talk phrases** such as:

- This will be a challenge.
- Just starting will be an accomplishment!
- It doesn't have to be perfect.
- I'll do a little at a time.
- I'll start now!

Many will understand the feeling
of accomplishment of washing dirty pots in
the morning that have been sitting in the sink all night.

What's the state of your office, your home, your car? In your office, do you have piles of files? Are you always in a hunt mode? Look around you. In your work area, are there stacks of paper, leaning towers of books, coffee cups, clothes? According to Brian Tracy, 90% of executives would not promote a messy person. However, some people believe it's output which is more important and that a neat desk is the sign of an idle mind. They may be kidding themselves. One lost file buried in paper rubble can be very costly.

Whatever it takes to help you feel organized is okay. Some people are happy with heaps of paper on the floor when they're doing a project, but major disorganization can create brain fog. You're likely to feel out of control and look disorderly. It been shown that you can increase your productivity by 20 - 40% just by cleaning your work area.

Five cleaning strategies for your office:

1. Remove all the piles of paper on your desk and put them into boxes. Ah, you can breathe again.

2. Work at 15 minute or half-hour increments whenever you can until the piles are sorted. Keep immediate work in upright containers on your desk; file the rest.

3. Sort through filing cabinets and remove those files that are not important to you now. Put them into cardboard boxes, label and store.

4. Organize the remaining paper files so that you can put your finger on one in a minute.

5. Organize computer files. If you cannot bear to delete any old folders or documents, copy them onto USB sticks and file in a safe place. Then delete them from your computer so it can work faster.

If you can't even face these five strategies, there are professional office organizers, available for an hourly fee, who will come into your home office or place of business and get your office better structured. They seem to have the temperament that allows them to love sorting through your scraps of paper. (For you that same task might seem as abhorrent as wading through bins of curbside trash!)

The Frazzled Woman Gets Organized!

If you want to become more focused, you'll need great organizational skills. Plan to use a large calendar or computer calendar and fill in all the activities of your work and personal plans. If you have a family, include their plans too.

A word of advice: Do not keep separate calendars for personal activities and work and family. **You will slip up!** With multiple schedules and the logistics involved, life can become very confusing. Sunday night is a good time to plan to set up the week.

Get rid of clutter in your home. Your mind will feel clearer. Bundle up your old books and magazines that no longer have meaning for you and give them to charity. Some women's shelter or youth shelter would be thrilled with your castoffs. Maintaining your organized space is your next challenge. Put books and papers away at the end of the day. Leave what needs to be worked on in the center of your desk. Be ruthless! Organizing your office, your car, your home, your schedule, will help you feel more in control, will help you achieve success or at least leave you feeling a whole lot better!

What's the state of your clothes closet and kitchen cupboards? Is dirty laundry piling up? Do you have too many junk drawers? The Chinese system of placement, Feng Shui, means harmony. It's the Oriental way of saying, "Everything has a place." And when items are in their appointed location, you can enjoy the harmony that comes with uncluttered rooms.

For those beleaguered women who do not have organizational skills in their genes, there are books on organization that can help you clean out your home, office, junk drawers, your briefcase and even your purse!

Waging War on Clutter:

"**CLUT-TER** To fill with scattered or disordered things that restrict movement or efficiency; a crowded or jumbled mass or accumulation; litter; disorder. Or, all the **stuff** you've got all over the place that everybody keeps telling you to get rid of".[18]

In the past, I was often frazzled and disordered until I learned organization from my husband. He would lay out his clothes each night: shirt, suit, socks, shoes, underwear and tie. In the early years of our marriage, I thought this practice was very amusing. But then one day it dawned on me that scrambling for clean shoes, pants, a matching jacket, a clean bra first thing in the morning was no laughing matter. **I finally caught on and realized the wisdom of simplicity.** If you are organized the night before, you will feel more focused and relaxed when leaving home. To further streamline the early morning rush, make lunch and bundle snacks, vitamins/minerals the night before. What a great way to start your day!

E-mail rules the day! A national survey reports that 85% of Canadians say that e-mail has made them more efficient in the workplace. A full 65% of those surveyed by *Ipsos Reid* said they'd rather communicate that way than by any other method. Electronic messaging has become a fact of life.

18 S. Culp, *How to Conquer Clutter*, Writer's Digest Books, an imprint of F&W Publications, 1989, p. 1

Even though the tone of voice previously heard in telephone conversations is lost in the printed word, still more than half of the people surveyed said they couldn't live without email. The trouble is that it takes a lot of time at the computer to keep up with work and personal e-mail, let alone jokes, surveys, junk mail and every advertisement that comes your way. Become proficient at using your Delete key more often. (You may want to save one or two jokes. After all, we all need to laugh to keep things in perspective!)

See if you can check and respond to e-mails at specific times during the day so that they don't eat into your time.

Don't let e-mail rule your life!

A special note for women with children: If you have young children and also hold a job outside the home, you'll have added chores and need to be super-organized, even if you have help. You'll still need to plan for meals, grocery shopping and doing errands. Otherwise, you'll likely feel scattered. While it's more common today for young couples to share home chores, surveys have shown that women juggle more roles than men. Often they have a heavier workload at home than men even if they too work outside the home. Women are usually the primary caregivers for family and health needs. Even those with a two-woman household will still need to divide chores. **Learn to delegate more, ask for help.** Even young children must learn to clean up their toys. Teach children how to make their own school lunches.

At the beginning of this chapter I asked you to imagine yourself as the time manager of your dreams, to put positive thoughts into action. Use some of the suggestions in this chapter and bring some semblance of organization and harmony to your life. You deserve it. After all, you too are a child of the universe.

Take-Away Gems

1. Slow down.
2. Stop dangerous or distracting multi-tasking.
3. Notice if you're an 'adrenaline junkie.'
4. Check your attitudes about what you have to accomplish in a day and seek to enjoy your moments.
5. Ditch overworking and set priorities for your life.
6. Plan some goals or even one goal that will keep you focused.
7. Don't procrastinate about tackling procrastination.

You're probably already wondering, "What happened to my Frazzled Hurried Self? Where did she go?" Bid her goodbye and thank her for her part in showing you that there's a better way to live. Don't worry, after a short while you won't miss her, as a new found part of you takes the lead to help you go from frazzled to fantastic!

CHAPTER TEN

Relationships
All We Need is Love...
and then some

She walked down the aisle trembling. Barely out of high school, this girl was making a pretty daring move to dedicate herself to a young man for the next 40 to 60 years. At the time, she wasn't even old enough to buy an alcoholic beverage or vote! He, at least, was three years her senior. Some would call it naïve or stupid, but in the early '60's, when you were in love, you got married. The star-struck couple stared into each other's eyes, he her gallant prince, she his princess. They had to be together. And yet there were nagging doubts that trailed her down that long aisle. Statistics mocked them both: most young marriages didn't last; couples needed to get an education, mature, establish a career, and gain some savings before making that lifelong commitment.

The young bride didn't know any co-habiting young couples. The 'Women's Movement' was just getting warmed up and didn't figure into most young women's lives at that time. She and her girlfriends sometimes remarked to each other, "This women's liberation thing is a really good idea". But the power of love and desire was too strong; hormones were surging. The choice was a walk down the aisle in a white dress.

That walk was mine. As a wedding ring was put on my finger, I said, "I do."

Over four decades later, I must say, with luck, sheer perseverance and determination, my husband and I are still together. As I look back, it appears to me that within our marriage, we've had many marriages. Of course we're not the same people as we were in those days. Thankfully, we've grown, changed, and matured as individuals and as a couple. Children test your mettle and make you grow whether you like it or not. A little counseling along the way has also been a boon. In many ways, long marriages can be the making or breaking of a person. One needs strength, wisdom, the ability to compromise, to reach out to one's partner, and the ability to curb one's temper!

We laugh a lot, so we must be doing something right.

My husband and I have been through an abundance of wonderful times as well as some unsettling times and many in-between times. It's been an enormous learning experience and both of us have mellowed considerably. I no longer slam kitchen cupboard doors when I'm angry (at least not very often); he no longer gives me the silent treatment for a few days at a time. Whew! We might get it right by our 50th wedding anniversary, but there are no guarantees! Fostering each person's development by being supportive is important. Yes, marriage and other types of cohabiting relationships are a lot of hard work, but the effort is necessary to make them happy. Couples need to remember the value of having fun together.

Love Still Makes the World Go 'Round

With the divorce rate at 50%, it's a wonder that anyone gets married anymore. Yet people are still tying the knot (mostly later in life than in previous generations). It seems that wedding cake is still a sought after dessert; whole bridal and honeymoon industries have sprung up around the event. Gowns are more elegant and more expensive than ever, while wedding-oriented rental halls and elegant banquet halls in museums or hotels proliferate.

Lavish dinners with champagne, including many bridesmaids in custom-made gowns, are still the norm. However, many couples once burnt by marital bliss now opt to live common-law. No rings, no ceremony, no muss, no fuss. Just give your loved one the key to your place and say, "Let's get on with it."

What Happened?

Everyone starts off 'lovey-dovey' and then anywhere from

days or weeks after the wedding to several decades later someone isn't 'in love' anymore. Actually I know a couple who said quits after 6 days and $30,000 later—it was a small wedding. Another couple split up at their 50th wedding anniversary party! I guess enough was enough.

Cindy, a friend of ours, left her parents' home after high school and went to study and live permanently in Europe. At that time, her decision seemed unbelievable, unheard of! Subsequently, Cindy had two failed marriages. It appears her independence didn't make much difference in terms of longevity of relationships. Perhaps she was ahead of her time; the state of relationships in those years couldn't support her early independence.

Everyone wants to feel loved and there's nothing worse than being dumped, especially by someone you love. Usual reasons cited are: couples grow apart, there's another woman (or many) or another man (or many), money squabbles, irreconcilable differences, the meddling parents or in-laws, the kids (they monopolize the woman's attention away from her resentful or jealous spouse), no sex, too much sex, no romance, no compassion, no companionship, or taking the person for granted. It could be that one or both of the parties is an alcoholic, drug addict or gambler. Perhaps one of the parties has a mental illness. Perhaps there's a special needs child that puts a strain on the weaker parent. There are couples who split up over the other's personal appearance or hygiene. Sometimes they simply grow away from each other, but truly, statistics tell us that money problems stand as the most common reason for divorce.

Value systems have to be 'in sync' for couples. If both believe in the same ideals, have a similar view of life, people and the world, these shared feelings can be important factors for a satisfactory relationship—although compatibility doesn't necessarily mean that couples have to be in the same business or industry.

> "Life has taught us that love does not
> consist in gazing at each other but in looking
> outward together in the same direction."
> — Antoine de Saint-Exupéry

Divorce: "It's not you, it's me." Divorce, as recently as two generations ago, was talked about in whispered tones; it was considered shameful and of course, what else, the woman's fault. Women were let off the hook if he was a 'womanizer' or gambler or drinker. Same sex marriages weren't even heard of and being part of a gay partnership was reason enough to get a person fired from a job or beat up. It does sound like the Dark Ages, but in reality a lot of changes have occurred in Western cultures in a very short time in history.

Cultural mores have changed enormously. In the early '60's, before the Feminist Movement began its real awakening, I recall my mother-in-law talking about a program she had seen on television about gay men. She was in shock; she had never heard of this lifestyle before. At that time, a large percentage of women were stay-at-home moms whose lives were expected to be centered on the home front and not on 'worldly' matters.

The common view was that it was shameful if a wife worked; it meant that a man "couldn't support" his family. Yet most marriages lasted. I'm not saying they all were blissful unions. Women in unhappy marriages stayed because they couldn't financially support themselves any other way. As well, both partners wanted to save face as there was a strong stigma attached to separation or divorce. In some cultures, this still is true.

So what changed? As always, youth changed the pace.

Young women in the next decade were beginning to choose education, careers and independence. The "Pill" and birth control information and devices were finally legally and readily available. Women suddenly had control over their reproduction and lifestyle. Strangely enough, even with today's open dialogue about sexuality, young girls still don't seem to know or understand their ripe fertility or Mother Nature's natural plan for them. Too many teens are getting pregnant, some we understand purposefully, and are blissfully unaware of the consequences of their frivolous adolescent decisions.

The continued industrial and the rapid technological revolutions also changed things forever. Women are staying in the workplace, starting their own businesses in droves, moving into positions of power in incremental yet progressive stages.

It's a New World (for some).

For some, equality might take longer. When a young man in his early 30's from another country told me that his sister had a baby boy, I tried to share in the moment by telling him about my new granddaughter, our first grandchild. His reaction was cool, pointing out that in his culture, having a boy as the first born was cause for great celebration. I explained what a great celebration we had for our little granddaughter as the first born, and that the whole family was overjoyed. My comments were greeted with a look of surprised disbelief—seemingly for our misplaced values.

New types of relationships with more openness, sharing and equality need to be forged. However, our species' treatment of women did not change very much for thousands and thousands of years. Therefore, I believe the blip of the last fifty or sixty years in history is merely a short transition period. There's still work to be done on the relationship (and equality) front.

Perhaps the best is yet to come. No man or woman is an island; we need each other. Frazzled Women somehow have to make time for their relationships with their partners, with their friends, with their co-workers. I believe that often they are barely surviving because they are preoccupied with chores on the home front while trying to build a successful career. By the time they climb up the stairs for bed at night, they want to sleep. Who can blame them? Yet they may be missing out, imagining they can just leave a partner on the shelf for when there's 'more energy' —and I don't mean just sex.

> *"Love has no desire but to fulfill itself.*
> *To melt and be like a running brook that sings its*
> *melody to the night. To wake at dawn with a winged*
> *heart and give thanks for another day of loving."*
> *– Kahlil Gibran*

Marriage or primary partnerships made today need to be a special bond and a safe sanctuary where each can be him/herself, a place where people truly love one another. We need to give our partner or spouse support when he/she is going through a rough time at work, with difficult relatives, with teenaged children, with illnesses, or with sick parents. Couples have to listen to each other, spend time with each other, hold hands, and caress each other. Each needs to let their partner know what's happening in their lives, even the small things, to keep connected. Most importantly, we need to remember what drew us to that person in the first place and build on that first strong bond. Perhaps nothing has changed after all.

We all know of the difficulties of growing numbers of women having to raise children alone and its devastating impact on children and society as a whole. The social order may have changed, but feelings haven't. People still need to be loved, to give love. Feelings still get hurt even while women are stepping up to equality.

How to Strengthen Your Primary Relationship

1. Be a good listener. That means let the other person speak without interrupting. Talk instead of fight. Don't keep repeating the same poor communication patterns if they're not working; something or someone has to change. Get appropriate help if you need to adjust interaction patterns; it could save your marriage or relationship. If you do most of the talking in the relationship, try being quieter and see if it encourages the other person to speak up more. If you're the one who doesn't talk much, see if you can articulate your feelings on more occasions. Think of the other's feelings, not just your own point of view. However, stand your ground for important issues, and know there are ways to get points across without being aggressive.

Love thy neighbor (and thy primary partner) as yourself.

---

2. Spend more time together, just the two of you. Go on dates together. Buy a present for each other once in a while or a meaningful greeting card or personal note. Phone each other during the day if you can, or send an e-mail. Talk about what excites you in life, what your passions are. If you love nature, take your partner to a lake, a forest, or a park. Likely, he/she will love it too. If he loves sports and you don't, accompany him to games sometimes; it could be fun. Encourage your significant other to go to one of your favorite fun activities.

3. Have fun. It's the glue that can hold a relationship together. There's something about laughing together that brings closeness. Often others wouldn't laugh at things the two of you find funny. It's very special, very personal, very bonding. Find something new to be interested in as a couple: dancing, boating, curling, bowling, and playing cards, going to the theater or the movies. Having mutual interests has been shown to keep couples committed to each other.

4. Allow no put-downs. Be careful not to put the other person down, especially in front of others, and let the other person know you don't like it if he/she gives condescending remarks to you.

5. Stop overspending. If you spend too much money, cut down or leave your credit cards at home. Decide on the way money is to be handled, whether you have your own account, his own account and/or a joint account. Let the better money manager pay bills. Money management (or mismanagement) is a significant problem for couples.

6. Don't shy away from physical contact: touching, hugging, kissing. This is not meant to make others around you feel uncomfortable; however, seek appropriate closeness. Talk about enhancing your sex life or get some books to help improve it if you feel this is an issue. If you do not have a satisfactory sexual relationship, this can be a symptom of other problems with the relationship (repressed anger or resentments). Or not having sex with your partner in itself can be reason for a poor relationship. It's no secret that men often lead with sex for closeness, but that women usually need to first have a feeling of intimacy with their partner before engaging in sex. I'm not sure why men and women were made this way, but somehow this very basic difference needs to be understood and worked on for better relationships. As people age, they may not want as much sex as they did when they were younger, but love in all its forms is what makes the world go 'round. Couples that do not have sex can begin to feel distant towards each other. Making an effort to revive a failing sex life can give a boost to primary relationships.

Please be aware: *If you are being battered, strengthening the relationship is not your priority.* Get professional help immediately. There are deeper and more urgent issues to resolve. If you use aggressiveness as an outlet or solution, I strongly recommend counseling to release and repair your anger.

May You Always Communicate!

Lorraine Weygman of *Weygman Consulting* (lorraine@weygman.com), who specializes in team building and interpersonal communication, says it is possible to take a successful approach to conflict.

Make sure you are aware of your communication strengths and weaknesses, as well as those of others. Are you the silent type who represses things that are bothering you until you explode with anger? Are you the aggressive type who blurts out what you're thinking and then has regrets? Do you know how to fight fairly by just concentrating on the issue at hand and refrain from dragging up other issues from the past? Do you or your partner give the silent treatment (shunning the other person) for 'punishment' of a perceived wrongdoing? Is either of you a yeller or screamer?

Whether the conflict is within yourself, or between you and another person, it's important to understand the origin and consequences of the feelings involved. Often we act irrationally toward another person because we are angry at ourselves. When we allow our anger to boil over without thinking of the consequences, we can say things we regret soon after.

Recognize patterns that precipitate day-to-day conflict

traps. Notice what triggers you or the other person and talk about it to see what you can do to change it.

Don't assume you know how a person feels. Check it out.

Which Type Of Communicator Are You?

Aggressive: Do you hurt or step on others when they express themselves? Do you dominate by making threats?

Passive or non-assertive: Do you get easily intimidated? Do you often put yourself down? Do you hide anger or do not respond in order to be liked? Most people who are passive or non-assertive have timid body language.

Assertive: These people exercise personal rights, speak up for themselves without denying the rights of others. They work towards equality in relationships. Assertiveness needs to be learned. It's not being aggressive. It's not being passive.

When being assertive, it's important to:
- Use direct eye contact and erect posture. This exudes confidence.
- Express your feelings comfortably. Present your honest emotions without hostile or whiny, martyred tones. Avoid leading with a "You" statement ("You never…You always….") Instead, use "I" messages which don't communicate blame ("I'm feeling left out and hurt when you don't let me know what's happening. I wonder if you don't trust me or don't like sharing with me. I really want to be part of your life"). Delivering blame and trying to incite a guilty response can seem like an attack. It invites flight or fight—undermining a calm resolution—whereas the "I" approach can encourage conversation without drawing a line in the sand for battle.

- Stand up for yourself with courage and conviction. If it's important enough to raise the topic, then you will need to be heard. Choose an appropriate time to broach the subject, and that does not include when you are feeling angry or irrational. Emotions can spoil reason.
- Know that there are non-verbal messages that often speak louder than words. Aggressive body language includes crossed arms, stiff body posture, hands on hips and tense facial muscles. Your best assertive stance is one that's composed and approachable. There are two sides to a situation: yours and that of the other person. Learn to understand how others are feeling merely by observing their body language so you can give off the message you want at the best opportunity and in the most successful way.
- Listen to others without talking over them (even if this is difficult for you!).
- If you can't mend the fences of your primary relationship, try getting professional counseling. Truly, relationship counseling is about self-growth and how two individuals can work together and compromise. For many, forgiveness will factor into counseling. Moving forward sometimes requires a forgiveness of self or forgiveness of the other person. The ability to forgive may be the turning point of whether couples can renew their relationship or end it.

Social Interaction: Relationships That Bind Us Together

Need to make new friends? Enroll in a program that interests you, whether to expand your field of expertise or to try something new. If you wish, you could pick up the knitting needles again; there are courses offered at many knitting supply stores.

If you like reading, find a book review club and meet people with like interests. If you love to dance, take up salsa dancing, folk dancing, ballet or other forms of dance classes that are often offered at community centers. Take up bridge, tennis, or volleyball. Join a walking club. Check out activities at your place of worship or join one.

Friends can help you live longer. Typically, women reach out to other women especially when under stress. Men often want to be alone. Yet it has also been shown that men who do have friends as they age also are happier and live longer.

"Many studies show that social isolation (i.e. not having social relationships) is a significant health risk factor. In fact, the negative health risk of not having friends is comparable to the health risks of smoking, having high blood pressure, being obese, or not getting enough physical activity."[19] "There is a growing body of research showing the importance of having positive relationships in our lives. In fact, the kinds of relationships as well as the number of social relationships we have greatly contribute to our overall mental and physical health."[20]

The Nurses' Health Study from Harvard Medical School found that the more friends women had, the less likely they were to develop physical impairments as they aged and the more likely they were to be leading a joyful life.

When we get busy, unfortunately we often let go of friendships. This is a mistake because women are such a source of strength to each other and can be a source of healing. "The hormone oxytocin is released as part of the stress responses in women. Oxytocin buffers the fight or flight response and encourages her instead to tend children and gather with other

19 Kiecolt-Glaser, J.K., McGuire, L., Robles, T.F., and Glaser, R. 2002,
    Psychoneuroimmunology: Psychological Influences on immune function
    and health. *Journal of Consulting and Clinical Psychology*, 70, 537-547

20 Ryff, C.D. and Keyes, C.L.M. 1995, The Structure of Psychological Well-Being
    Revisited, *Journal of Personality and Social Psychology* 69, 719-727

women. Studies of this tending or befriending response suggest that more oxytocin is released to produce a calming effect."[21]

Make time to see each other if you have moved away or at least communicate by mail, e-mail or telephone. Don't drop the communication. Small things matter—a little note, a kind word; we all need it. If you both live in the same area, plan time with a friend for dinner or lunch. True friends love to listen to you and to hear what's happening in your life. Even if they can't solve any problems for you, you'll feel better just airing your feelings or laughing together.

I can still hear the cackling laughter in my head of my mother and two of her sisters, years after they have passed on. Each Saturday afternoon, they gathered at one of their homes for 'tea and sympathy.' Often other female family members were invited and those afternoons were marked on the calendar as though they were important doctors' appointments—only more fun! The atmosphere was warm and inviting and created a bonding of relationships that was never broken. They talked about the week's events, told jokes and traded advice about children and husbands. Even though economic times were tough, they found many things to laugh about. For my mother, I know that those afternoons were restoring, and the highlight of her long work week.

---

*Do not underestimate the healing power
of women socializing with other women.*

---

21 "Biobehavioral responses to stress in females: Tend-and-befriend, not fight-or-flight". Taylor, Shelley E.; Klein, Laura Cousino; Lewis, Brian P.; Gruenewald, Tara L.; Gurung, Regan A. R.; Updegraff, John A. *Psychological Review*, Vol 107(3), Jul 2000, 411-429

Feelings, Nothing More Than Feelings

Getting in touch with one's feelings is a good exercise. When we're busy or frazzled, the main feelings we likely recognize are frustration and fear. We may feel frustrated that we never seem to have enough time for the things we need to do or want to do. We may fear that life/time is slipping away from us; we're not quite in control.

There's a huge range of emotions between those that give a positive glow and those which cause hurt. Recognize your feelings when you feel them. Don't stuff them or pretend they don't exist, especially the negative ones. Hiding or suppressing them causes emotions to get locked in the body. Those who research, study and write about psychoneuroimmunology (PNI), such as Candace Pert, PhD, neuroscientist, believe that these locked (unresolved) emotions cause physical illness because the mind affects the body. Express your unhappy emotions in a healthy manner; talk them out, cry, feel them. Then you can deal with their hold on you.

Negative feelings can steer our behaviour and our communication with others right off the tracks. There is good reason for counting to 10 before reacting because emotion can block good sense. In each of the following situations, a) imagine your worst response and then b) envision your best rational approach:

- Your child failed a term. You may feel worried, confused, angry, out of control, frustrated.
- You're waiting at an instant bank teller machine. The line-up is long and it isn't instant. You may feel angry, impatient, anxious (if you're late), helpless, powerless.
- You talk about someone in a bad light and you find out this same person overheard the conversation. You may feel embarrassed, anxious, ashamed, or sorry for the hurt

you may have caused. If you're the person that was talked about, you may feel angry, hurt, crushed, pained, dejected.

- You get a phone call that your teenage child has become very ill while he is travelling abroad on a youth tour. You may feel fearful, terrified, panicky, alarmed, paralyzed. You become focused on getting him home.

On the job, at home, in public, and on the road, we encounter situations every day that incite feelings within. Most don't require any action on our parts, but there are some that can be life-altering and require a steady guiding hand. At the time, we seldom see or feel the benefits of difficult situations. A young woman loses her job or her marriage ends. She is devastated. It's hard to see initially, but such difficult events can be the start of a new and better direction.

Joyfulness for happy events—a wedding, the birth of a baby, buying a new house—all need to be celebrated. The event is often that much more pleasurable because we have tasted and known the opposite, the depths of despair.

For relationships to work, strengthen your feelings by acknowledging them. Love deeply, laugh loudly, live with purpose and hope, and you can't go wrong. Relationships function on communication; smooth performance depends on continued dialogue from both sides. Often, compromise oils the gears.

Take-Away Gems

- Be a good listener.
- Spend more time together. Find mutual interests and have fun.
- Support each other. Refrain from putting each other down.

- Make a concerted effort to keep your purchases within your budget.
- Be affectionate. In some way, keep your physical relationship alive.
- Be aware of your own and others' communication styles. Find those that work.
- Air feelings in a healthy manner.
- Keep other friendships alive.
- Get counselling for self growth and healing of relationships. Sometimes ending them is the only way people can survive. But first, give them your best shot.

Frazzled Woman, you'll need to slow down to make time for relationships, for loving, for self-growth. I know you can do it. Self-growth is also self-love. You'll need to look at the relationship you have with yourself. Do you self-nurture? Do you like or love who you are? If not, seek change as the best bargain you'll ever encounter.

> *"If your passion does not*
> *include yourself, it is not complete."*
> — *Buddha*

Women are resilient, strong, determined and make enormous accomplishments. We were born with qualities and gifts that can reveal themselves at any time in our lives, even in old age! If we seek these wonderful qualities within ourselves, we will find that they were there all along.

Embrace relationships. They will warm you.
Perhaps one will even keep you cozy on a cold night.

Love Reawakened

Icicles melt from around my heart.
As the cold numbness thaws,
It leaves a blissful joy
That warms
My body and mind.

Tenderness and understanding
Rush back to fill empty depths,
So that being alive
Becomes greater than surviving.

I begin to share my hurts and delights
With one who will listen
And feel,
And our souls blend in perfect harmony,
Each singing its very own song,
Yet touching glorious tones
In the other.

Love that was dormant,
Frozen in indifference,
Is being reclaimed and polished
To a promising new brightness.

And now
The glowing sunlight
Of our re-awakened love
Rises steadily in the morning sky.

While as two separate beings
We enjoy our own identities
And bask in the radiant dawn
Of each other.

by Rosalie Moscoe

CHAPTER ELEVEN

Menopause!
A change like no other

Women live through hormonal changes although for many, not without difficulty.

Who said being a woman was easy?

'The Change' Is it hot in here or *what?*

It was a cool spring day, uneventful, a day off work, and my girlfriend and I were shopping at a mall. Suddenly, my heart started to pound wildly; I was experiencing a sensation of impending doom. No one else seemed bothered; people were walking by in their rushed everyday fashion. Another strange feeling started coming over me. It wasn't hot outside, I wasn't blushing, but this intense feeling of heat started to engulf me, my chest, my arms, my neck, my face. Panicked, I blurted to my friend, "Get me to a hospital!"

Her answer was quite calm. "Don't get yourself in a flap. It's just a hot flash."

A hot flash? A hot **what**?! This can't be happening to me!

(Pause for a moment here and mimic the song, **Jealousy**. If you are of menopausal age, you will probably remember Frankie Laine and the melody):

Menopause, it's taking over me
Can I resist it, can't I just miss it
Menopause, hot flashes and sleepless nights
Oh how it warms me, but now I'm born free.

About 70 million women in North America are entering the climacteric or are in the midst of the change of life. Lord help us all!

We baby boomers must have youth at all costs. And the costs are demanding—my husband calls it "high maintenance," and it includes facials, manicures, hair coloring, wads of makeup, lipsticks, powder, creams to lift, creams to rejuvenate, creams to take years off our faces and to remove cellulite from our panty lines. When the 'girls' (a fond term for women over 50) and I get together, we dare each other about who's going to get a face lift first. So far, no one's had the nerve.

The Sandwich Generation

Many of us have teenagers or adult kids moving back home on one side and aging, ailing parents on the other.

> We're the slab of meat getting pressed
> by two slices of heavy, sourdough bread.

Cultures differ in their attitudes toward women in menopause. In India, mature women are respected; in Africa they are revered for their wisdom. In China, women hardly have any signs of menopause and most pass through it uneventfully. By contrast, in North America, for years we've been considered 'over the hill.' However, perhaps that adage is fading. With the many role models of mature professional women working as CEO's, managers, engineers, architects, teachers, artists, performers, and politicians, society is finally learning to respect and appreciate the contributions made by wise, stable individuals of both genders.

Stress at Menopause

A set of symptoms can result from stress at menopause. Some ailments at this time of life are directly attributed to the cessation of menstrual cycles. Physical symptoms that commonly occur during pre-menopause (during a woman's mid-forties) might include hot flashes, vaginal dryness, joint pains, headaches and indigestion. This occurs due to the waning of estrogen and other hormones. The ovaries are losing or have lost the ability to produce eggs and estrogen.

We cannot forget that this phase of life signifies an end to an extremely important part of a woman's life.

Susan Ballinger, psychologist, feels that around the time of the menopause many women suffer increased environmental pressures. Menopause symbolizes the beginning of old age in a society where sexual desirability and social worth are strongly equated with youth, vitality and beauty. Tension is increased by having a spouse who is also passing through a similar insecure stage of life. Yet today's women have a much longer life expectancy than past generations and they now have choices about what to do with the rest of their lives. Most women are now more positive (and excited) about the post-menopause phase of life.

While physical changes are happening to us as we age, psychological ailments may take hold as the 'hormone dance' swings us up the scales and back down. Stress and hormonal influences often precipitate forgetfulness, panic attacks, anxiety and depression. According to Scottish psychologist Gerald Greene, psychological complaints may be traced to high levels of stress including the departure of children, which may be difficult for some women to deal with. (Even so, many are quite happy at this event!) Perhaps women at this stage of life have had enough stress throughout their lives and can't cope as well as they did earlier. It appears that depression can be attributed to hormonal changes and ongoing life stresses.

Reducing stress using the many means presented in this book can help women cope with menopause. Yale University researchers have found that stressful situations, in which the individual has no control, were found to activate an enzyme in the brain called protein kinase C - which impairs the short-term memory and other functions in the prefrontal cortex, the executive-decision part of the brain. Feeling in control is the key element. Taking control of one's health is a good first step.

Another reason for depression at menopause can be attributed to common nutritional deficiencies. Eating well is crucial and will help make this passage for women much smoother. Reducing sugar and junk food is vital to one's health and coping abilities.

Are You Losing it?
Super Nutrition at Menopause

Feed your brain. Memory-enhancing foods are those that nourish your brain to help it keep up with the demands of your body. The most reliable way to protect brain cells is to eat fruits and vegetables. They're brimming with antioxidants to protect aging cells against damaging free radicals—elements that break down cells.

All fruits contain antioxidants. The top five antioxidant fruits, however, are blueberries, blackberries, cranberries, strawberries and raspberries. The best vegetables include kale, spinach, Brussels sprouts, spinach, garlic and broccoli. Again, all vegetables help repel age-related diseases.

B-Complex vitamins work in chorus to promote the health of the brain and immune systems by protecting nerve tissue against oxidation. They enhance memory and insulate nerve cells. Besides meat and other protein foods, there are many good vegetarian sources of B vitamins, including whole grain pasta, grains, rice and wheat germ, dark green vegetables, mushrooms and nuts. Vitamin B6, pyridoxine, helps long-term memory. Foods containing B6 include whole grains, cereals and breads, spinach, bananas, liver and avocados.

Protein-rich foods such as beef and chicken are brain boosters which contain Tyrosine, an amino acid. Other amino acids found in yogurt, turkey and low fat milk increase mental alertness and assist the body and brain in times of stress. Tryptophan, an amino acid found in whole grains, has a calming effect on the brain.

Essential Fats are good for the brain, especially as we age. Cold water fish such as salmon, mackerel, anchovies, sardines, herring and Atlantic sturgeon are primary sources of healthy fats. Flax seeds are great fiber sources and contain Omega 3 fats.

Phosphatidylcholine found in soy products and lecithin readily converts to acetylcholine, the memory neurotransmitter in the brain. There are some forms of choline available in supplement form.

Boron is a semi-metallic element that helps our attention and memory. It is found in raisins, apples, nuts and avocados.

Zinc is an essential mineral that enhances memory and concentration. It can be found in seafood, oysters, fish, legumes, cereals, whole grains, and dark-meat turkey.

Iron enables red blood cells to deliver oxygen throughout the body. Enjoy it in leafy vegetables, raisins, peanut butter, eggs, liver, shellfish, lean meats, soybeans and molasses.

A multivitamin and mineral supplement provides you with a good nutritional base and has been shown to improve mood in both males and females.[22] Especially helpful for memory, mood and brain efficiency are Vitamin E, Vitamin C, Folic acid, Lipoic acid, and CoQ10. Folic acid, B6 and B12 are necessary to promote normal homocysteine levels. There's growing evidence that homocysteine plays a key role in brain (and heart) health.[23] Phosphatidylserine (PS), a phospholipid substance, is a major building block for brain membranes. PS has been

22 *Neuropsychobiology*, 1995, 32:2, 98-105, Benton D; Haller J, Fordy J., Dept. of Psychology, University College Swansea, UK
23 *The H Factor Solution*, Braly, M.D., Holford, P., Basic Health Publications Inc. 2003, pgs 167-183

proven to boost energy and electrical activity across the entire brain. Some memory formulas for enhancing brain health are available at good pharmacies and health food stores.

Let's Remember the Positives!

There are bonuses attached to this time of life—no more worries about accidental conception, the new freedom when children find their way securely into adulthood, and the joy of becoming a grandmother. Those who have better coping abilities and better perceptions of stress have shown fewer and less severe psychological symptoms at menopause. The transition into life's next phase can be beautifully filled with certainty and self-assurance, or it can be laden with stress. The power lies in how one handles this particular Change.

To bring excitement at this time of life and to keep your brain making new neural connections, it may be the time to take up something new. Take piano or golf lessons, learn a new language, travel, or take classes in international cuisine. Keep your memory stimulated while sitting quietly with games like Suduko or crossword puzzles. A friend of mine became a marathon runner; another climbed Mt. Kilimanjaro. Others I know started new businesses. Single people find new partners. Many write books, explore family history or indulge themselves in groups that share interests such as gardening, investing, calligraphy or art.

The Menopause Remedies

There were always home remedies for menopause. In the early years of the 20th century, ladies could purchase Lydia E. Pinkham's magic vegetable compound formulated for their 'special' ailments. Women loved it. Turned out, it contained upwards of 20% alcohol! No wonder they appreciated it. It surely elevated their libidos and improved their outlooks . . . albeit temporarily. (The Food & Drug Act of 1929 legislated obvious changes to the formula.)

As for my own 'malady' I thought a trip to the doctor was in order. He said (and did I detect a note of amusement at my common, unoriginal condition), "Take these pills and you'll feel like a new woman." He even gave me a month's free samples. I accepted his offer of Premarin and marched to a pharmacy counter where I learned that they were made from the urine of a pregnant mare. Oh?

Now that's when I began to think that we women aren't very bright. I mean, how many men do you know who would take a pill made from something found on a barn floor? I asked the pharmacist, "Will I start 'neighing,' or will I get an overwhelming urge to go galloping into the night? Will the smell of hay send me into a state of euphoria? Will I get teary-eyed when I see little ponies? And when someone asks me my age, will I reply with a thump, thump with my leg?" (These are things a woman has to know if she's going to take a pill made from the urine of a pregnant horse.) The pharmacist just stared at me. But I was menopausal. What did he expect?

Sensing that someone had to be serious, he began listing possible side effects such as cancer, stroke, and a few other little goodies. I walked out of the drugstore and threw the pills in the nearest garbage can. (Good thing I did. A few years later, disturbing statistics made the news about the dangers of these 'wondrous' hormones.) My next stop was at the library to get information about natural remedies and natural hormones made from soy beans and wild yams. Somehow the thought of soy beans and wild yam cream didn't make me fearful.

My continued search for relief took me to acupuncture

and natural herbs. I decided that 5,000 years of the practice of acupuncture in China was a sufficient track record for me, but when I found myself sitting in the office of a doctor of Chinese medicine and acupuncture, I was disappointed. She wasn't Chinese at all, and she had a British accent. She asked, "Why are you here?" to which I replied, "I feel like a rusty old car that needs my motor 'revved' up." She nodded, and then proceeded to stick little needles in my arms and legs. Suddenly, the room started to spin around me. I felt faint. She tried to reassure me. "Don't worry," she smiled. "In my 10 years of practice no one has ever fainted on me." I was sure I would be the first one. (I have since had acupuncture with positive results and no ill effects.) After a series of cold towels on my head, she sent me off to a Chinese herbal market to pick up my ration of twigs, roots, mushrooms and other unfamiliar products. At least the herbalist was Chinese. He gave me strict instructions how to boil and strain the brew, but warned me about the terrible taste.

At home I stirred the concoction in a pot on my stove and gagged at the smell. How was I going to drink it? I felt like one of the witches in Shakespeare's *Macbeth*. **"Double, double toil and trouble, fire burn and cauldron bubble . . . eye of newt and toe of frog . . ."**

Finally, the elixir was ready and a humorous song provided me with the courage to swallow it. As the old "Love Potion #9" line goes, **'I held my nose, I closed my eyes— I took a drink!'**

Immediately, I ran to the mirror to see if I had morphed into a young maiden. No such luck. (I told you I was menopausal—a little 'off center' as my mother used to say!) My British/Chinese herbalist had told me I would have to drink the noxious brew for at least a month and that it would help my libido too. (Speaking of libido, my friend says she'd rather have a good hamburger.) Libido? Did I remember what that was? Actually a few days later I did start to feel better, more like a 54 Chevy rather than a 1915 model T Ford. And for that I was thankful! I suppose it's all in the attitude.

Natural bio-identical hormones for menopause and their symptoms are in the spotlight and the cause of war between pharmaceutical companies and natural medicine. Books like *The Sexy Years* by Suzanne Somers or Diane Schwartzbein, Uzi Reiss, Christine Conrad, John Lee, Jonathan Wright and mine have opened the door to successful long term treatments with bio-identical hormones for thousands of women whose lives have permanently changed for the better…Bio-identical hormones are molecularly different from synthetic hormones. They are prescription medications, unavailable over the counter. They are FDA approved and have been in use for more than 25 years. The only physicians who know about them are self-taught and have done their own research to find the abundant scientific data on them (My own library houses more than 100 articles from conventional medical publications on the benefits of bio-identical hormones and their successful and safe usage since the early 1980's).

The missing link can easily be found in the following piece of information. The pharmaceutical industry does not have patents on bio-identical hormones since they are formulated to look exactly like the molecules of hormones that occur in nature. This means less money for the particular pharmaceutical company since the product made to order by the compounding pharmacy or lab can conceptually be easily duplicated.

Oprah Winfrey's website regarding her show in January 2009 features information about bio-identical hormones. Many other research reports give detailed information as to the safety and efficacy of these natural hormones.

Many doctors prescribe them for patients and have compounding pharmacies make them specifically for each patient. The FDA is testing them, but it seems there is no final word on the subject. After the WHI (Women's Health Initiative) that struck down the safety of HRT (hormone replacement therapy), there was much controversy about those hormones, which were supposed to have been a 'wonder' treatment for women approaching menopause. However, the synthetic hormones made from pregnant horses' urine and other concoctions showed dangers for women's health—breast cancer, heart attacks, thrombosis and more.

Scientists began testing hormones found naturally in the human body and discovered that in **correct** dosages they could relieve not only menopause symptoms, but also other age-related ailments such as osteoporosis, cancer, and heart attacks. While still in use and growing in followers, bio-identical hormones are in dispute at this time. Issues are being raised about standardizing hormone replacement as dosing is still in a trial and error stage. However, this is a positive development due to the fact that each woman is unique and requires a dosage particular to her metabolism and her symptoms. Synthetic hormones' dosages are mostly 'one size fits all.' A variety of dosage forms run the gamut from capsules to suppositories, sublingual drops and transdermal creams. Even when there seems to be some consistency in using a topical ointment, there are different bases used; some of these bases are better tolerated by women than others. Many doctors start at a low dose and gradually increase until symptoms of hot flashes and night sweats are relieved. The maintenance dose is that which is the lowest to provide relief of symptoms and a good quality of life. The problem of high dosing without a break seems to be an issue and many doctors cycle patients on and off the hormones. Many pros and cons are also discussed on the blog site of Dr. Jeffrey Dach, MD, jefferydach.com.

Before using these hormones, I suggest women do their homework and speak to their family doctors or gynecologists. You can also find doctors who treat using bio-identical hormones and book an interview appointment before deciding what is best for you. To locate these doctors, many women seek out pharmacies that prepare these compounding formulas and learn from them which doctors prescribe bio-identical hormones. Many over-the-counter weaker preparations (such as wild yam cream) and herbal remedies, vitamins and minerals are also available for menopausal symptoms. For further help, naturopaths can provide guidance in this area.

Check with complementary/alternative doctors, naturopaths or other qualified health care providers. Being proactive is important. I suggest you do your research.

Sexual Changes at Menopause

There's also the reality of diminishing sexual needs or waning of desires, sometimes for the woman, the man or both. Either couples do something to work on this issue or don't bother. For those who don't bother, the situation may lead to divorce. However, many couples don't make an issue about lowered sex drives and stay committed because of comfort, their family or true love and devotion for one another. Others may decide it's in their best interests to work on reviving their sex drive and there are doctors who can help. While we've all heard about hormonal help for women (either synthetic or natural), some doctors will test for hormonal deficiencies in men and also prescribe hormones for them. Again, pharmacies that specialize in compounding may have lists of doctors participating in bio-identical prescribing.

'The Change' and Frazzled Husbands

My poor husband wasn't sure what to make of 'The Change.' He said, "There should be a course for men called, **How to Cope with Wives in Menopause.**" I don't know what he was complaining about. I told him I was feeling "free, wild and crazy." To alleviate his concerns, I donned a slinky black dress, a bright pink feather boa and fixed him with a provocative stare. Surely, I thought, he'd rejoice in my new energy.

In answer, he simply raised an eyebrow and asked, "Are you going to the grocery store dressed like that?"

Men.

In every home with a menopausal woman, windows are flying up and down. It's always too hot, too cold! Feeling hot and then chilled is tricky business and can even spark battles. You've heard of *Star Wars*; at our house it's called **Thermostat Wars**. Every summer, I keep the air conditioner on, even on cool days. My husband complains, "It's freezing in here." He turns it off. But then, after he falls asleep, I jack up the air conditioning again. Aah... cool and comfortable! He wakes up the next morning, shivering.

I now think of hot flashes as power surges and appreciate how good they feel on a cold **winter's** day.

And if all that personal adjustment isn't annoying enough, there's this insidious little invader that creeps up on you when you least expect it, when you're standing in front of a crowd of people giving a speech, or when you're all dressed to go to a wedding, or when you're posing for a family portrait. It's about **those little hairs**. Hair is supposed to sprout on your head, legs, eyebrows and other less talked about places of the body but not on one's chin! Everything else I can endure, but not hairs popping up in broad daylight on my face! We have to keep on plucking and finding ways to deal with them: creams, electrolysis, laser treatments, anything else we can endure because like weeds, they insist on returning.

There's something liberating about being in one's 50's (or 60's). I'm not afraid to speak my mind anymore. If a waiter serves me cold food in a restaurant, someone tries to butt in my line, someone tries to put me down, or makes a crude remark in public—watch out! Spouses often have to catch up with these emerging new personality traits in their wives, but most adapt well enough. This may be the time for a renewed relationship if you truly want to stay together as life partners.

To get through menopause more easily, realize that this time of life is an opportunity for introspection, a time to get to know yourself a little bit better. It's also a good excuse for fewer commitments, and more rest and relaxation. Yes, we're getting older and to accept this stage is in fact sobering. (Weren't we just kids playing skipping games in the street?) Yet when we accept and truly live, and love, while being 'in the moment', our days can become more meaningful, exciting and liberating. Consider the post menopausal years as a transformation.

Take-Away Gems

1. Appreciate and accept menopause as a time of wise maturity and stability.
2. Consider physical symptoms as temporary. Seek helpful natural remedies and/or medical care.
3. Use superior nourishment for stress relief at menopause.
4. Remember the positives: fewer responsibilities, freedom of fear of conception.
5. Learn something new and challenging to bring excitement to your days.

Formerly Frazzled Woman, recognize menopause as a time of renewal and transformation. Suddenly, you are a multi-hued butterfly, ready to spread your wings for new adventures. In your own way, you can fly!

In 1991, I was scheduled to give a concert for all the children at Sunnyview Children's Center in Toronto, Canada. Many of the children there were in wheelchairs or on crutches and most were visibly disabled. Some, I was told, wouldn't live out the year.

The school had received my children's record albums beforehand and the students had learned the songs. I asked their teacher which one the children liked best and she said *The Rainbow Song*. Of all the many thousands of children I had performed to, no other group had ever said that was their favorite. The day of the concert came and the children gleefully sang along with all my songs during my performance.

I had been a bit apprehensive wondering how I was to get through the concert without tears streaming down my cheeks. I was doing okay. It was the last song and I announced that I'd be singing *The Rainbow Song* and whoever would like to join me on stage could come forward and sing it with me. They all cheered and en masse they trudged up to the front of the room with their crutches or in their wheelchairs. Mostly teachers and very few children were left in the audience—only those who were totally immobile, some in beds.

The 50 or so children lined up on both sides of me and the music started and they sang at the top of their lungs: **There's a rainbow glowing inside of me, there's a rainbow here everyday. Oh there's a rainbow glowing inside of me and it feels like it's here to stay!** Tears flowed down my face, not because I felt sorry for them, but because their humanity and sensitivity touched me. Their robust enthusiasm also taught me about their heightened awareness of life's meaning.

Those children knew there was a rainbow, a light, perhaps their spirit glowing brightly inside of them. And they felt it strongly.

We each own a rainbow glowing inside. Sometimes we don't feel it because we've become overwhelmed, burned out. You too can find and know the light of that rainbow, that innate excitement for living.

I wish you much success in your life. May you find peace, love, good health, strength, laughter and fulfillment in all the wonderful things you dare to dream about. You have enormous potential to enjoy a healthy, stress-free life. You're stronger than you know.

To the Frazzled Hurried Woman

I hope that the ideas and tips I have shared with you in this book will charge your spirit. I challenge you to embrace change—even in baby steps—to achieve your own healthy, happy balance. Dark clouds and rain may come into our lives, but the sun always shines again and often brings forth a spectacular rainbow. May the next one be yours.

Please e-mail me at rosalie@healthinharmony.com to let me know how you got started on your wellness path and whether you faced any stumbling blocks. You can also connect with me via my social media networks at www.healthinharmony.com. Share your successes so that we can rejoice together.

The Frazzled Woman's Recap Points

1. **Assess your commitments.**
   Review your commitments and decide what you can do to protect yourself against being overburdened. Pare them down and/or enlist help. Do not think you can do it all yourself.

2. **Realize that stress response starts with your perceptions of events.**
   Become aware of the root causes of your stress. Try to alter your perception of challenging events and your reactions to them. Positive self-talk bolsters your self-esteem and confidence.

3. **Notice if your glass is half empty or half full.**
   Shake off the victim role. Live in an atmosphere of gratefulness.

4. **Learn to relax.**
   Practice deep breathing techniques. Listen to music that you love. Get a massage or soak in a tub. Slow down and be more mindful of all your actions, especially when driving.

5. **Assess your healthy balance.**
   Assess your state of health on The Wellness Wheel. Discover your strengths and start improving your short-falls. Get outdoors. Don't forget about prayer. Schedule a doctor's appointment if you're not feeling well or go for an annual check-up.

6. **Visit your health trio: exercise, sleep and nutrition.**
   Find time to stay fit. Make sleep a priority for better health. Rest when you're tired and don't feel guilty about it. Learn about superior nutrition to revive strength and well-being.

7. **Give your brain and body super nutrition.**
   Eat breakfast. Try not to skip lunch. Bolster immunity, energy and mood with foods that are rich in vitamins and minerals.

8. **Bring back the hearth to your home.**
   Get comfortable again with home cooking. Stock your kitchen with fruits and vegetables, raw nuts, olive oil and protein foods and reduce junk food, caffeine and sugar intakes. Collect dietary-specific cookbooks and use them. Pack nourishing snacks and drink 6-8 glasses of water throughout the day. Your body will thank you.

9. **Re-evaluate your use of time.**
   Organize the week in advance so that there is time for YOU each and every day whether it's for exercising, deep breathing, listening to music, resting or walking around the block. This is a MUST.

10. **Rekindle the fire in your relationships.**
    Carve out some time for you and your primary partner at least once a week—without children in tow. Find time to talk to each other and practice loving attentions. If you can't work out relationship issues, get professional help. Maintain contact with friends. Look for reasons to smile and laugh.

11. **See Menopause as a time for reflection, wise maturity and stability.**
    Learn something new to bring excitement to your days and treat yourself well. You deserve it!

It's all about quality of life, not longevity.

Count to ten. Relax. Calm down.
Be content, seek
Balance.

MANAGING STRESS

8 Weeks to Optimum Health Andrew Weil, M.D.

90 Days to Self-Health C. Norman Shealy

Bonkers Dr. Kevin Leman

Celebrating Anger Angela Jackson

Goodbye To Guilt Gerald G. Jampolsky, M.D.

Healthy Pleasures David Sobel, M.D., Robert Ornstein, PhD.

Healthy Travel Marlene Coleman, M.D.

How to Conquer Clutter Stephanie Culp

I'm Okay, You're Okay Thomas A. Harris, M.D.

Love, Medicine & Miracles Bernie S. Siegel, M.D.

Managing Stress E.J. Neidhardt,

Menopausal Years, The Wise Woman Way Susan S. Weed

Minding the Body, Mending the Mind Joan Borysendko, PhD.

One Minute for Myself Spencer Johnson, M.D.

Positive Imaging Norman Vincent Peale

Seeking Your Healthy Balance
       Donald A. Tubesing & Nancy Loving Tubesing

Stress Management Walt Schaefer

Take Charge of Your Health Carolyn DeMarco, M.D.

The Art of Dealing with Rejection and **Breathing Room —
       Creating Space to Be a Couple** Elayne Savage, PhD.

The Dance of Anger Harriet Goldhor Lerner, PhD.

The Hurried Woman Syndrome Brent Bost, M.D.

The Joy of Stress Peter Hanson, M.D.

The Power of Now Eckhart Tolle

The Relaxation Response Herbert Benson, M.D.

The Type E Woman Harriet B. Braiker, PhD.

Timeshifting Stephan Rechtschaffen, M.D.

Transitions: Making Sense of Life's Changes William Bridges

Wellness Workbook John W.Travis, Regina Sara Ryan

What We May Be Piero Ferrucci

When I Say No, I Feel Guilty Manuel J. Smith, PhD.

Women's Burnout Dr. Herbert J. Freudenberger, Gail North

Write Your Own Pleasure Prescription Paul Pearsall, PhD.

NUTRITION FOR WELL-BEING

Brain Allergies W. H. Philpott, M.D., D.K. Kallita, PhD.

Fats that Heal, Fats that Kill Udo Erasmus

Get The Fat Out Victoria Moran

Good Fat, Bad Fat Louise Lambert-Lagace, Michelle LaFlamme

Guide to Eating Out Michael R. DeBakeyk, Antonio M. Gotto, Jr.,
Lynne W. Scott

Healing Schizophrenia A. Hoffer, M.D. PhD.

Is This Your Child Doris Rapp, M.D.

Live Longer Feel Better with Vitamin B3 A. Hoffer, M.D. PhD.,
H. Foster, PhD.

Optimum Nutrition for The Mind Patrick Holford

Orthomolecular Nutrition for Everyone A. Hoffer, M.D. PhD.,
Andrew Saul, PhD.

Syndrome X Jack Challem, Burton Berkson, M.D., Melissa Diane Smith

The Diet Cure Julia Ross, MA

When Food Is Love Geneen Roth

Additional Supportive Services by Rosalie Moscoe

1. Keynote Addresses and Workshops for companies, associations, hospitals, government, mental health agencies and community groups
2. Small Group Coaching on stress, nutrition via Teleclasses, Webinars
3. One-to-one Nutritional Consulting in person
4. One-to-one Nutritional Consulting telecoaching
5. Free bi-monthly e-zine Health in Harmony News
6. Rosalie's Blog: www.healthinharmony.com

Further Information can be found at:
www.healthinharmony.com

Toll-Free Number: 1-877-653-0077